Anonymus

Memorial of Thomas Ewing, of Ohio

Anonymus

Memorial of Thomas Ewing, of Ohio

ISBN/EAN: 9783741142352

Manufactured in Europe, USA, Canada, Australia, Japa

Cover: Foto ©Thomas Meinert / pixelio.de

Manufactured and distributed by brebook publishing software
(www.brebook.com)

Anonymus

Memorial of Thomas Ewing, of Ohio

MEMORIAL

OF

THOMAS EWING,

OF

OHIO.

NEW YORK:

THE CATHOLIC PUBLICATION SOCIETY,

No. 9 WARREN STREET.

1873.

THIS MEMORIAL, into which are gathered, for preservation, the tributes of respect and love offered to the memory of a great man, together with testimony regarding a higher blessing than earthly honor and renown, is prepared with tender reverence and filial devotion.

AN AUTOBIOGRAPHICAL SKETCH,

WRITTEN IN 1869.

THE following sketch by the late Thomas Ewing will be read with new interest since the recent decease of that great man.—*Cincinnati Commercial.*

"My father settled in what is now Ames township, Athens County, early in April, 1798. He removed from the mouth of Olive Green Creek, on the Muskingum River, and the nearest neighbor with whom he had association was, in that direction, distant about eighteen miles. There were a few families settled, about the same time, on or near the present site of the town of Athens, but no road or even pathway led to them; the distance was about twelve miles. There was also an old pioneer hunter encamped at the mouth of Federal Creek, distant about ten miles. This, as far as I know, comprised the population statistics of what is now Athens County. I do not know

1

the date of the settlement in what was called
No. 5—Cooley's settlement—it was early.

"At the time of my father's removal, I was
with my aunt, Mrs. Morgan, near West Liberty,
Virginia, going to school. I was a few months in
my ninth year. Early in the year 1798, I think in
May, my uncle brought me home. We descended
the Ohio River in a flat-boat to the mouth of
Little Hocking, and crossed a bottom and a pine
hill along a dim foot-path, some ten or fifteen
miles, and took quarters for the night at Dailey's
camp. I was tired, and slept well on the bear-skin
bed which the rough old dame spread for me ; and
in the morning my uncle engaged a son of our
host, a boy of eighteen, who had seen my father's
cabin, to pilot us.

"I was now at home, and fairly an inceptive
citizen of the future Athens County. The young
savage, our pilot, was much struck with some of
the rude implements of civilization which he saw
my brother using, especially the auger, and expressed the opinion that with an axe and an auger
a man could make everything he wanted except a
gun and bullet-moulds. My brother was engaged
in making some bedsteads. He had already finished
a table, in the manufacture of which he had used
also an adze to smooth the plank, which he split in

good width from straight-grained trees. Transportation was exceedingly difficult, and our furniture, of the rudest kind, composed of articles of the first necessity.

.   .   .   .   .   .

"We had wild fruits of several varieties, very abundant, and some of them exceedingly fine. There was a sharp ridge quite near my father's house, on which I had selected four or five service or juneberry bushes that I could easily climb, and kept an eye on them till they should get fully ripe. At the proper time, I went with one of my sisters to gather them; but a bear had been in advance of me. The limbs of all the bushes were brought down to the trunk like a folded umbrella, and the berries all gone; there were plenty still in the woods for children and bears, but few so choice or easy of access as these. We had a great variety of wild plums, some exceedingly fine—better, to my taste, than the best tame varieties. I have not seen any of the choice varieties within the last thirty years.

"We of course had no mills. The nearest was on Wolf Creek, about fourteen miles distant; from this we brought our first summer's supply of bread-stuffs. After we gathered our first crop of corn,

my father instituted a hand-mill, which, as a kind
of common property, supplied the neighborhood.
after we had neighbors, for several years, until
Christopher Herrold set up a horse-mill on the
ridge, and Henry Barrows a water-mill near the
mouth of Federal Creek.

"For the first year, I was a lonely boy. My
brother George, eleven years older than I, was too
much a man to be my companion, and my sisters
could not be with me generally in the woods and
among the rocks and caves; but a small spaniel
dog, almost as intelligent as a boy, was always
with me. I was the reader of the family, but we
had few books. I remember but one besides
'Watts's Psalms and Hymns' that a child could
read—'The Vicar of Wakefield,' which was almost
committed to memory; the poetry which it contained, entirely.

"Our first neighbor was Capt. Benjamin Brown,
who had been an officer in the Revolutionary war.
He was a man of strong intellect, without much
culture. He told me many anecdotes of the war
which interested me, and, among other things that
I remember, gave an account of Dr. Jenner's then
recent discovery of the kine-pox as a preventive
of the small-pox better than I have ever yet
read in any written treatise, and I remember it

better than any account which I have since read.
He lent me a book—one number of a periodical
called the 'Athenian Oracle'—something like our
modern 'Notes and Queries'—from which, however,
I learned but little.   I found, too, a companion in
his son John, four years my senior, still enjoying
sound health in his ripe old age.

"In 1801, some one of my father's family being
ill, Dr. Baker, who lived at Waterford, eighteen
miles distant, was called in.   He took notice of me
as a reading boy, and told me he had a book he
would lend me if I would come for it.   I got leave
of my father and went, the little spaniel being my
travelling companion.   The book was a translation of Virgil, the Bucolics and Georgics torn out,
but the Æneid perfect.   I have not happened to
meet with the translation since, and do not know
whose it was.   The opening lines, as I remember them, were—

> "'Arms and the man I sing who first from Troy
> Came to the Italian and Lavinian shores,
> Exiled by fate, much tossed by land and sea,
> By power divine and cruel Juno's rage;
> Much, too, in war he suffered, till he reared
> A city, and to Latium brought his gods—
> Hence sprung his Latin progeny, the kings
> Of Alba, and the walls of towering Rome.'

"When I returned home with my book, and for

some weeks after, my father had hands employed in clearing a new field. On Sundays, and at leisure hours, I read to them, and never had a more attentive audience. At that point in the narrative where Æneas discloses to Dido his purpose of leaving her, and tells her of the vision of Mercury bearing the mandate of Jove, one of the men sprang to his feet, declared that he did not believe a word of that—he had got tired of her, and it was all a made-up story as an excuse to be off; and it was a d——d shame after what she had done for him. So the reputation of Æneas suffered by that day's reading.

" Our next neighbors were Ephraim Cutler, Silvanus Ames, William Brown, a married son of the Captain; and, four or five miles distant, Nathan Woodbury, George Wolf, and Christopher Herrold : and about the same time, or a little later, Silas Dean, a rich old bachelor, Martin Boyles, and John and Samuel McCune. Mr. Cutler and my father purchased ' Morse's Geography,' the first edition, about 1800, for his oldest son, Charles, and myself: it in effect became my book, as Charles never used it, and I studied it most intently. By this, with such explanations as my father gave me, I acquired quite a competent knowledge of geography, and something of general history.

"About this time, the neighbors in our and the surrounding settlements met and agreed to purchase books and to make a common library. They were all poor, and subscriptions small, but they raised in all about one hundred dollars. All my accumulated wealth—ten coon-skins—went into the fund, and Squire Sam. Brown, of Sunday Creek, who was going to Boston, was charged with the purchase. After an absence of many weeks, he brought the books to Capt. Ben. Brown's in a sack on a pack-horse. I was present at the untying of the sack and pouring out of the treasure. There were about sixty volumes, I think, and well selected; the library of the Vatican was nothing to it, and there never was a library better read. This, with occasional additions, furnished me with reading while I remained at home.

"We were quite fortunate in our schools. Moses Everett, a graduate of Yale, but an intemperate young man, who had been banished by his friends, was our first teacher; after him, Charles Cutler, a brother of Ephraim, and also a graduate of Yale. They were learned young men, and faithful to their vocation. They boarded alternate weeks with their scholars, and made the winter evenings pleasant and instructive. After Barrows's mill was built at the mouth of Federal Creek, I, being the mill-boy, used to take my two horse loads of grain in the evening, have my grist ground, and take it home in the morning. There was an eccentric person living near the mill whose name was Jones (we called him doctor); he was always dressed in deerskin, his principal vocation being hunting; and I always found him in the evening, in cool weather, lying with his feet to the fire. He was a scholar, banished no doubt for intemperance; he had books, and, finding my fancy for them, had me read to him while he lay drying his feet. He was fond of poetry, and did something to correct my pronunciation and prosody. Thus the excessive use of alcohol was the indirect means of furnishing me with school-teachers.

"My father entertained the impression that I would one day be a scholar, though quite unable to lend me any pecuniary aid. I grew up with the same impression, until, in my nineteenth year, I almost abandoned hope. On reflection, however. I determined to make one effort to earn the means to procure an education. Having got the summer's work well disposed of, I asked of my father leave to go for a few months and try my fortune. He consented, and I set out on foot next morning, made my way through the woods to the Ohio River, got on a keel-boat as a hand at small wages, and in about a week landed at Kanawha salines. I engaged and went to work at once, and in three months satisfied myself that I could earn money slowly but surely; and on my return home in December, 1809, I went to Athens, and spent three months there as a student, by way of testing my capacity. I left the academy in the spring with a sufficiently high opinion of myself, and returned to Kanawha to earn money to complete my education. This year I was successful, paid off some debts which troubled my father, and returned home and spent the winter with the new books which had accumulated in the library, which, with my father's aid, I read to much advantage. I went to Kanawha the third year, and, after a severe summer's labor, I returned home with about six hundred dollars in money, but sick and exhausted. Instead, however, of sending for a physician, I got "Don Quixote," a recent purchase, from the library, and laughed myself well in about ten days. I then went to Athens, entered as a regular student, and continued my studies there till the spring of 1815, when I left, a pretty good though an irregular scholar. During my academic term, I went to Gallipolis, and taught school a quarter, and studied French. I found my funds likely to fall short, and went a fourth time to Ka-

nawha, where in six weeks I earned one hundred
and fifty dollars, which I thought would suffice,
and returned to my studies; after two years' rest,
the severe labor in the salines this time went hard
with me.

"After finishing my studies at Athens, I read
Blackstone's 'Commentaries' at home, and in July,
1815, went to Lancaster to study law. A. B.
Walker, then a boy of about fifteen years, accompanied me to Lancaster to bring back my horse,
and I remained and studied law with Gen. Beecher.
I was admitted to the bar in August, 1816, after
fourteen months' very diligent study—the first six
months about sixteen hours a day.

"I made my first speech at Circleville the November following. Gen. Beecher first gave me a
slander case to study and prepare. I spent much
time with it, but time wasted, as the cause was
continued the first day of the court. He then
gave me a case of contract, chiefly in depositions,
which I studied diligently, but that also was continued. A few minutes afterward, a case was called,
and Gen. Beecher told me *that* was ready; the jury
was sworn, witnesses called, and the cause went
on. In the examination of one of the witnesses,
I thought I discovered an important fact not noticed by either counsel, and I asked leave to cross-

examine further. I elicited the fact, which was decisive of the case. This gave me confidence. I argued the cause closely and well, and was abundantly congratulated by the members of the bar who were present.

"My next attempt was in Lancaster. Mr. Sherman, father of the general, asked me to argue a cause of his, which gave room for some discussion. I had short notice, but was quite successful, and, the cause being appealed, Mr. Sherman sent his client to employ me with him. I had as yet got no fees, and my funds were very low. This November I attended the Athens court. I had nothing to do there, but met an old neighbor, Elisha Alderman, who wanted me to go to Marietta to defend his brother, a boy, who was to be tried for larceny. It was out of my intended beat, but I wanted business and fees, and agreed to go for $25, of which I received $10 in hand. I have had several fees since of $10,000 and upwards, but never one of which I felt the value, or in truth so valuable to me, as this. I went, tried my boy, and he was convicted, but the Court granted me a new trial. On my way to Marietta at the next term, I thought of a ground of excluding the evidence, which had escaped me on the first trial. It was not obvious, but sound. I took it, excluded the evidence, and acquitted my client. This caused a sensation. I was employed at once in twelve penitentiary cases, under indictment at that term for making and passing counterfeit money, horse-stealing, and perjury. As a professional man, my fortune was thus briefly made."

BIOGRAPHICAL SKETCH.

BY HON. HENRY STANBERY.

THE following biographical sketch was written some years ago by my father's dear friend,
Hon. Henry Stanbery, and was republished in the
Cincinnati *Commercial* immediately after my
father's death.—E. E. S.

The family of Thomas Ewing resided, prior to the
Revolutionary war, near Greenwich, Cumberland
County, New Jersey, where the old family mansion is
still to be seen. George Ewing, the father of the subject
of this sketch, was born there in 1754. In 1775, he
enlisted in the New Jersey Line, where he obtained the
rank of lieutenant. He was present at the battles of
Germantown and Brandywine, and spent the winter of
1777 at the memorable camp of Valley Forge. While in
the army, he sold, on credit, the property which had
descended to him, and, when his bonds became due, was
paid in Continental money, then a legal tender, though
rapidly depreciating, and which soon after became totally
valueless. Thus reduced in circumstances, he removed to
the western side of the Alleghanies in 1786, and settled

on a small farm near West Liberty, Ohio County, Virginia, where Thomas Ewing was born on the 28th day of December, 1789.

In April, 1792, the family removed to the mouth of Olive Green Creek, on the Muskingum River. In the year 1795, the Indians rising in all directions, they were obliged to take refuge in a block-house at Olive Green, to avoid the danger of being massacred. An elder sister had taught young Ewing to read; and, while he was in the garrison, he very assiduously cultivated acquaintance with almost the only book it afforded—the Bible—and acquired therefrom the cognomen of Bishop, which clung to him for many years.

In 1797, he was taken to West Liberty, and there went to school about seven months; at the expiration of which time he returned to his father, who had then removed to the waters of Federal Creek, into what is now Athens County, Ohio. The spot selected by his father was then in the wilderness, and seventeen miles beyond the frontier settlements. Here, for nearly three years, they were shut out from any intercourse with the world. Young Ewing, during this time, read the " Vicar of Wakefield " and " Fool of Quality." These and the Bible were all the books which, up to that time, he had been able to procure. In the year 1800, a few other families from New England had settled on Federal Creek; and, in the winter of that year, a school was opened under the superintendence of Chas. Cutler, a Cambridge graduate, who was succeeded by Moses Everett, from the same college.

Ewing studied, one quarter under each, the rudiments of a common English education, and this was the total of his schooling until 1812. This little enterprising community of New Englanders that were then settled upon Federal Creek had but few books; and, to procure a further stock, they formed a library association, and raised a small fund by subscription. This literary fund (in all probability the first that was ever formed in the Northwestern Territory) was sent to one of the Eastern cities, and invested in books.

The whole collection was brought across the mountains on horseback in a sack. With the exception of Goldsmith's works, the books were not well selected, consisting principally of the novels then fashionable, such as "Amanda," the "Romance of the Forest," and dull treatises on controversial doctrines of divinity. Subsequent additions were made to the library, among which were Plutarch's "Lives," Stewart's "Philosophy," Darwin's "Zoonamia," and Locke's "Treatise on the Understanding."

Young Ewing fell upon these with a literary avidity which none can understand but those who, under like circumstances, have felt it; and he devoured the whole, reading at all his leisure hours, and principally at night by the light of hickory-bark.

From the age of thirteen, the life of Ewing was laborious. Then he became a substantial assistant to his father upon his farm, and by-and-by he had the principal management of it. Still, he found time to read, as all can find who have a thirst for knowledge; but, as he grew older, he had less time to read than when a boy. The little he had learned, however, but influenced him with a desire of learning more. The love of knowledge was the prevailing and all-absorbing passion of his soul. To be a scholar was then the summit of his highest ambition. He felt that he had acquired all the knowledge within his reach; but this only taught him how little, in fact, he knew, and was far from allaying his burning thirst for knowing more. Knowledge there was, he knew, but how to reach it was more than he could tell. Poverty stared him in the face. The father and his farm anchored him at home, but his buoyant spirits led him off on a thousand plans—through many aerial castles, and in many delightful visions. Calculations were made, but made in vain. Plans were formed, but they were soon but air. A world was abroad, but what it was the eager student hardly knew. And yet, the more he knew of it, the more he panted to act his part in it. But the more he thought of his situation, the more he despaired. Reflection at last ripened into actual suffering. His feelings became intensely interested. The bitter, melancholy conclusion at last was that he must abandon all hopes for ever.

But in the summer of 1808, he was awakened from this stupor by a youth nearly of his own age, whom his father had hired for a few months to assist him in farming, and who had rambled about and seen much of the world. The narrations of this young man, and many of his adventures, awakened Ewing; and as money was what he wanted—in order to obtain the means of pursuing his studies—he was induced to go with him to the Kanawha salines, in Western Virginia, in order there to try his fortunes.

He obtained the consent of his father, and left home early in August, with his knapsack on his back, and but little spending-money in his pocket.

He got on board of a keel-boat at Marietta, bound for Kanawha, and made his way to the new El Dorado of his imagination. During the three or four months he was absent, he worked as a common hand at the salt wells, and was tolerably successful; but the greatest satisfaction he had was that he could do something in future.

He returned home in the winter, with about eighty dollars, the amount of his wages, leaving his companion behind, whose roving disposition prompted him to rove still more. This money Ewing gave to his father, to assist him in paying for his land. The surrender of this little and hard-earned treasure to his father for the purpose of enabling him to save his land from forfeiture was no ordinary sacrifice, as it postponed for a year all prospect of prosecuting his studies, and condemned him, for a while, to stifle the high hopes he then nourished in his bosom.

Early in the spring of 1809, Mr. Ewing set out again for the Kanawha salt-works. The whole of this season, until November, he spent in most assiduous labor, and

3

he succeeded well—the profits of the season being about
four hundred dollars, out of which he appropriated sixty
to pay the balance due on his father's land. He spent
the winter at Athens, then a flourishing academy, but
irregular in the course of studies, as it left the student
to pursue such a course as he might think proper. At
the end of about three months, he left this academy, and
returned to Kanawha, after receiving there such encouragement from the president of the institution, and such
a stimulus from others, as fixed his determination to procure the means of obtaining an education. The next
two years he devoted to this object; and he returned
from the Kanawha in November, 1812, with about eight
hundred dollars in money, and with his health considerably impaired with severe hard labor.

This sum he supposed would be sufficient to enable
him to go through the preparatory studies, and acquire
a profession. His health, however, was so much injured
that he was unable to commence his studies. But he
again fell upon the library in the neighborhood of his
home, which was now enlarged; and, from the repose
given him, and the leisure spent in reading such works
as Don Quixote, he laughed himself into such good
health and spirits that in December he was able to go
back to Athens, where he continued to be a most indefatigable student until the spring of 1814. His progress
during this time was very rapid. He became familiar
with many of the best English authors; and, as his judgment matured, he easily obtained a knowledge of the

English grammar, rhetoric, and logic. Mathematics, however, was his favorite study, for which he had a natural inclination, and hence Euclid was the favorite author. The philosophy which depended upon mathematical demonstration he studied with care and pleasure, and in it made much proficiency.

He also studied the Latin, but determined to omit the Greek.

In 1814, Mr. Ewing became satisfied that his funds would not hold out, and he took a school in Gallipolis.

Not liking this employment, at the end of a quarter he relinquished it, and returned to Kanawha, the old scene of his labors, to collect a small sum that was due him, and to see what could be done toward adding something to his funds. He threw off the dress of the student, and again went to work at the salines. He hired a furnace, and in one month of incessant toil, the severest he ever undertook, he improved the state of his finances so that he felt confident they would bear him through his studies.

At some period of his labors at the Kanawha salt-works—and it was probably this—he labored twenty hours out of the twenty-four, and he was often found, during the four hours allotted to sleep, working with open eyes, but still asleep, between the two rows of boiling salt kettles, where a false step would probably have destroyed life.

With his hard-earned treasure, he returned to Athens, where he continued till the spring of 1815.

At the examination in May, 1815, the trustees of the institution rated him the degree of A.B., being the first, with one other, upon whom this degree was conferred by a college in Ohio.

The circumstances which decided Mr. Ewing's choice of profession were probably these. In 1810, he took a boat-load of salt to Marietta. While there, accident led him to the Court-house. The Court of Common Pleas was then in session, and he entered a court-house for the first time in his life. It happened that an interesting criminal trial was going on. The attention of the young salt-boiler was .riveted to the scene; nor did he quit the room until the case was closed. He had witnessed a high intellectual effort—he had listened to an advocate (the late Elijah B. Merriam) of uncommon ability.

Hitherto he had not known or felt the power of eloquence. We may suppose that, along with his admiration of intellect in another, there was associated a consciousness of his own mental powers, and a feeling kindred to that which caused the untutored Correggio, after gazing for the first time upon the pictures of Raphael, to exclaim: "I, too, am a painter." In truth, this must have been so, for he turned away to pursue his toilsome occupation with the fixed purpose of becoming a lawyer.

After he left college, he spent a few days with his relatives, and then began his legal studies in the office of General Beecher, at Lancaster, Ohio—a man of sense and intelligence, and for several years a member of Congress from Ohio.

Gen. Beecher discovered the merit and approved the efforts of Mr. Ewing. He received him as a student in his office, and, immediately upon his admission to the bar, took him into partnership. While Mr. Ewing was pursuing his law studies, he was an indefatigable student, devoting to his books every hour that was not required for necessary repose.

Mr. Ewing's rise at the bar was rapid. He entered almost immediately into full practice in his region of the State. In keeping with the generous filial character he displayed in the appropriation of his first savings at Kanawha, he expended his first accumulation at the bar in the purchase of a fine tract of land in Indiana, on which he settled his father and family. As his powers and reputation grew apace, the area of his practice was extended to embrace and was chiefly confined to the Supreme Court of Ohio, the Circuit Court of the United States for the District of Ohio, and the Supreme Court of the United States at Washington, in which he has been engaged with only occasional interruptions by high official duties down to a recent time. He was distinguished at the bar for his sound logical mind, a clear conception and mastery of the general principles that underlie the system of the law, and a most comprehensive power of analysis and array of the facts bearing upon his case; to which may be added an extraordinary general knowledge of the round of physical sciences—

great power in the hands of a lawyer, which has contributed its share in placing him in the front rank of the profession in the United States.

Mr. Ewing finished his collegiate studies at so late a period, and was for some years thereafter so constantly devoted to his practice, that his attention was not early turned to political concerns. He entered upon political life in his election in 1830 to the Senate of the United States. Without family or political influence or affiliations, his election to this high place was prompted by a strong and just sense of his eminent qualifications, honorable alike to the Legislature and the new Senator.

In no period since the formation of the Government has the Senate Chamber been graced by a galaxy of minds more brilliant and powerful than in the first term that Mr. Ewing sat there. Webster, Clay, Calhoun, Benton, Wright, Preston, and other first names in the nation then filled the Senate, and it is no slight praise to say that the Ohio Senator lost nothing in the contrast; the reputation that won for him the place was but augmented by the new theatre on which his powers were displayed. He bore a not inconspicuous part in the exciting political contests of the sessions from 1830–37 as an opponent of the administration of General Jackson.

Under the operations of the strict party discipline, gaining force year by year, Mr. Ewing failed of a re-election, and at the end of his term resumed the full practice of his profession.

On the accession of General Harrison to the Presidency

in 1841, Mr. Ewing was next called into public service by the invitation of the incoming President to a place in the Cabinet. The general voice of the country designated him as the proper man for the organization of reform in the administration of the important department of the General Post-Office, but he was ultimately assigned to the more conspicuous and important place of the Treasury. The death of General Harrison brought Mr. Tyler into the Presidency, and, on his special invitation, the Harrison Cabinet remained in office, until the developments of the memorable extra session of 1841 disclosed to the world the violation on the part of Mr. Tyler of all the pledges of the party that elected him to power, and the disappointment of the hopes grounded on its success.

Mr. Ewing was prompt among his associates in the Cabinet in his election between an adherence to the principles and promises of his party on the one hand, and the allurements of place and power on the other; and the scathing letter of resignation with which he surrendered the keys of office did much to mark the boundaries that separated the President from the true men of the party he had betrayed.

In the formation of the Cabinet of General Taylor, in 1849, by common voice a prominent place was assigned to Mr. Ewing. With a just appreciation of his qualifications for the important task, he was invited by the President to the charge of the new Department of the Interior, involving in its administration, beyond the ordinary duties of a Cabinet officer, the organization of a new department of many separate bureaus, and having charge of the public lands, the Indian affairs, and the Patent Office. He filled this post with honor and ability until August, 1850, when, after the death of General Taylor and the accession of Mr. Fillmore, the Taylor Cabinet, failing to harmonize on certain important questions with the new President, resigned their offices.

Mr. Ewing was thereupon appointed by Governor Ford to a seat in the Senate (vacated by the resignation of Governor Corwin, who went into Mr. Fillmore's Cabinet), and continued in the Senate until March 4, 1851, when he retired from political life, and resumed the practice of his profession.

In person, Mr. Ewing was large and stoutly built, so that he was physically as well as intellectually a strong man. In his early hard labor in felling the forests of the West, and in feeding the furnace of the salt-works, his figure must have been developed and strengthened much more than if in early life he had been devoted wholly to sedentary pursuits; and at the same time he was confirmed in habits of industry that he never lost.

His manner of speaking was not graceful, yet it commanded attention. He was powerful from his matter rather than his manner. Plain, open, straightforward, fearless, with little or no attempt at oratorical display, he laid hold with all his might upon whatever his hands found to do. His eye was fixed upon a point, and it was impossible to swerve him. Others there were more eloquent in manner than he, to whom nature had given finer voices or more captivating oratory; but few were more powerful in thought, few with more resources, or who had more or better weapons in any logomachy tilt. He seemed to be well informed on every point that arose in debate, whether a matter of history, of philosophy, of poetry, or of criticism, thus showing that he had read much, and had not read in vain.

How instructive is the life of such a man, and with what force does it commend itself to every young American, not only arousing him to exertion, but admonishing him to fix his ambition high, and to gratify it only in the path of virtue, integrity, and honor, and thus to win that reputation that abides and outlasts the corrosive rust of time!

Honors ever seek him in the virtuous days of a republic who deserves them; but that is not honor which is won by meanness and intrigue at the cost of integrity and self-respect.

Grovelling ambition tarnishes and stains whatever it touches; but an ambition like that which animated the bosom of Ewing dignifies and ennobles whatever it wins.

DEATH OF HON. THOMAS EWING.

Special to the Enquirer.

LANCASTER, OHIO, October 26, 1871.

Hon. Thomas Ewing died at his residence in this city at three and a half o'clock this afternoon. All his sons and daughters were with him, and he retained his faculties almost to the last moment.

Funeral services will take place on Saturday next, at eleven o'clock. The remains will be interred in our cemetery.

"Such grand old age, crowning a happy life,
As makes men pause, and wonder why they thought
Springtime so beautiful."

FUNERAL OF THOMAS EWING,

AT LANCASTER.

Correspondence of the Cincinnati Commercial.

LANCASTER, OHIO, October 28, 1871.

THE funeral of Thomas Ewing, the most honored citizen of this city, took place to-day from St. Mary's Roman Catholic Church, in the presence of one of the largest assemblies of prominent and distinguished men ever seen in Fairfield County upon any public occasion.

For several weeks before he died, Mr. Ewing calmly awaited the final dissolution, and, although subjected at times to the most severe suffering, endured the ordeal with heroic fortitude, and retained possession of his extraordinary faculties to the last. His beloved daughter, the wife of General Sherman, was with him some time before his decease, and fondly hoped to take him to her home in Washington, where she could devote herself without a sense of divided duty to his remaining days; but the lapses of suffering were too short to permit the

execution of the cherished purpose, and, on Thursday
last, surrounded by all he held dear on earth,

> —— " full of repentance,
> Continual meditations, tears, and sorrows,
> He gave his honors to the world again,
> His blessed part to heaven, and slept in peace."   .

The remains, encased in a superb burial-casket, lay in
Mr. Ewing's sitting-room, in the family residence, and
were viewed by friends and visitors for the last time up
to the hour of burial.   Everything in the room appeared
as he left them; his table, with books, papers, and
writing materials, his watch and spectacles, all lay as
deposited by his hands when the final summons came.
Fine portraits of the distinguished statesman as he
appeared in early, middle, and after-life hung upon the
walls, and Jones's magnificent colossal bust, well known
to every Ohioan, and pronounced by every one who
knew the original to be the best likeness which the hand
of art has produced, stood near, and told more eloquently
than words of the intellectual greatness that made Mr.
Ewing the fit compeer of Webster, Clay, and Calhoun.

Lying in the cold embrace of death, the once commanding countenance and the towering form still indicated the physical greatness of the man.   The features
wore a solemn, dignified, and calm expression; the noble
brow and the massive " dome of thought " riveted attention, and in their splendid proportions gave the imagination scope for endowing the clay with all the grand

intellectual attributes that inspire respect and excite admiration.

A rich simplicity characterized the preparations for entombment. There was no ostentation, no attempt at worldly display. Some loving hand had placed sweet flowers and fragrant leaves upon the coffin-lid, the plate of which bore the simple inscription:

THOMAS EWING.
Born December 28, 1789.
Died October 26, 1871.

The last look was taken at the house, and before removal the final enclosure of the casket was performed.

The train from Columbus at ten o'clock brought Governor Hayes; Hon. F. B. Pond, Attorney-General of the State; Hon. Isaac R. Sherwood, Secretary of State; Adjutant-General W. A. Knapp; General Charles C. Walcutt, Collector of the Seventh District; Rev. A. G. Byers, Secretary of the State Board of Charities; Honorables McIlvaine, White, and Welch, Judges of the Supreme Court; Senators John Sherman and A. G. Thurman, of Ohio; Judges James L. Bates, John L. Greene, and Joseph Olds; John H. James, Esq., of Urbana; L. J. Critchfield, Esq., Reporter of the Supreme Court, and several other prominent citizens.

Judge William B. Woods, of the United States Court in Alabama, and Hon. Willard Warner, ex-Senator of Alabama, were also in attendance; and Professor Gibbons, of the Ohio University, came to pay the final tribute of respect to one whom that institution honored as its first graduate.

The residence was filled with friends and visitors. All the bells in the city tolled during the funeral.

At eleven o'clock, the burial cortége moved from the house to St. Mary's Church. The casket was borne to the church—only a square distant—by the pall-bearers, and was received at the entrance of the sacred edifice by his Grace Archbishop Purcell, of Cincinnati; Very Rev. Father Young, of Washington, D. C., and other assistant clergymen. The pall-bearers were: Governor R. B. Hayes, of Ohio; Honorables Henry Stanbery, of Cincinnati; Senators A. G. Thurman and John Sherman; Judge Welch, of the Supreme Court; John II. James, of Urbana; George Reber, of Sandusky; A. B. Walker, of Athens; II. B. Curtis, of Mt. Vernon; W. Marshall Anderson, of Circleville; C. B. Goddard, of Zanesville; II. H. Hunter, M. A. Daugherty, John T. Brazee, J. D. Martin, James R. Pearce, D. Tallmadge, Charles Borland, G. G. Beck, S. A. Griswold, F. A. Foster, Samuel Herr, C. M. L. Wiseman, Jacob Beck, and J. F. Vandemark, Esquires; and Dr. T. O. Edwards, of Lancaster.

The mourning carriages conveyed Judge P. B. Ewing; Generals Hugh, Thomas, and Charles Ewing, sons of the deceased; General Sherman and Colonel Steele, married to daughters of Mr. Ewing, and their respective families.

The imposing ceremony of the Catholic Church provided for the burial of the dead was celebrated by

Father Young, after which Archbishop Purcell ascended the pulpit, and addressed the immense congregation Not all the Archbishop said reached the hearing of the reporter, but enough was gathered to ascertain that an eloquent eulogy was pronounced. The life and career of Mr. Ewing were intelligently and graphically traced, from the earliest period down to the last moments, and the record was held up as a model for the young and an honor to the surviving relatives.

There was a beautiful manifestation of Providence, the Archbishop said, in the presence of Father Young, the nephew of Father Fenwick, afterwards the first Bishop of Cincinnati, who celebrated the nuptials of Mr. Ewing, and who has himself been his warm personal friend for more than half a century, manifestly sent by Almighty God to reach out his hand to his dying friend, and help him in his last step into the church, and to soothe his dying hours. He had always treated the other denominations with uniform respect, especially the Methodist denomination, which he respected for its many good works; but in the Roman Catholic faith alone he found consolation, and, for a period of thirty-eight years, Mr. Ewing had been deeply convinced that the Catholic Church was the only one that contained satisfying evidences of the truth of the Christian religion. He was a frequent and for a considerable period of his life a constant and reverential attendant at the ministrations of the Roman Catholic Church, and down to the very last year of his life took personal care to see that his name was borne on the list of pew-holders in the church.

"Never," said the speaker, "was he heard to utter an objection to its ritual, its morality, or its influence on governments or on society. This influence he had deeply studied in Guizot's 'History of Civilization,' in 'Balmes,' in the 'History of the Religious Orders of the Catholic Church,' in the sublime devotion of the 'Sisterhoods of Charity,' in the life and virtues of his incomparable wife, and the education of his children.

"Once in Boston he desired to hear the elder Channing, but on that occasion he was disappointed. The Unitarian pulpit was occupied by a mediocre, an uninteresting speaker. The congregation was composed of a few worshippers, if they could be so called, reclining listlessly in luxurious pews. But on his return to his hotel, he passed by a Catholic church, too small for the congregation, many of whom were kneeling on the wet ground, apparently in fervent prayer.

"The scene, the incidents of the day, had their effect on the thoughtful mind of Mr. Ewing, who related to me himself this anecdote. It helped, with other and graver considerations, to convince him where the true religion could be found.

"More than once, especially at the earnest request of Mrs. Ewing and his daughter, Mrs. Sherman, I availed myself of what I regarded as auspicious occasions to urge him to embrace that saving faith to which I had often heard him render unmistakable testimonies. His answer was,

'Not now.' After all, faith is a gift of God, but it is granted to the sincerity of the enquirer, to purity of life, to moral worth, to the untiring prayer of the just. It was therefore granted to our deceased lamented friend.

"On the Saturday before his death, he sought my ministration, and, in the fulness of the faith, with marked reverence and devotion, received at my hands the body and blood of Jesus Christ in the sacrament of the Holy Eucharist. 'He that eateth my flesh and drinketh my blood hath everlasting life; and I will raise him up in the last day.' "

In gratitude for the assistance which the church had rendered Mr. Ewing in raising his family in the right way, he directed before his death that a thousand dollars be given for religious purposes, and this was only part of the many benevolent acts of his life. He had given two thousand dollars toward the erection of the church in which his remains were then receiving the last rites, and he had in every proper manner acknowledged himself in will a Catholic, as well as he did in form before he died. And it was because the Catholic Church embraced everything in its faith to satisfy the reason, the intellect, and the heart, that Mr. Ewing came into its fold. He was convinced that the Holy Scriptures sanction and point out everything the church believes and teaches. "Yes," repeated the venerable prelate, "the holy Bible is the charter of our faith and the rule of our life. The holy Bible, which is to be found in every Catholic family, and which is read by every

Catholic, is not forbidden or prohibited, as the enemies of the church and religion falsely charge. It is the foundation of Christianity, because it is the Word of God, and the Catholic, the universal Church, so teaches."

The Archbishop, in conclusion, paid a glowing tribute to Mr. Ewing as a statesman, as a patriot, as a citizen, father, and friend, and recalled his first impression of him seated in the United States Senate, surrounded by the great ones of the greatest country in the world, feeling then, as his riper knowledge of the man confirmed, that in that most distinguished and august assembly he occupied a fitting place. Mr. Ewing, he said, disapproved of secret societies, such as the Masonic and Odd Fellows and others, simply because he considered them unnecessary. This was a free country, and such organizations were really useless. The church afforded every means and opportunity for the exercise of benevolence in every form, and what was the need for darkness and secrecy?

Mr. Ewing had shown by a spotless life of eighty-two years that the teachings of religion were enough to enable any man to lead a blameless life, become rich and honorable, and bequeath to his posterity the still richer inheritance of a good name, without the assistance of a secret society.

Such was his moral purity, the Archbishop said, that he never was heard to utter a profane or vulgar word, and such was the example of his life that his memory was honored in his loving and devoted children.

At the close of the ceremonies in the church, the funeral procession reformed in the following order:

1. Pall-bearers,
2. The hearse,
3. Family and relatives,
4. Distinguished citizens from abroad,
5. Members of the bar,
6. City Council,
7. Citizens,

and proceeded to the cemetery, about half a mile out of the city. The remains were deposited beside those of Mrs. Ewing, whom her distinguished husband survived only a few years, and the interment was final.

And thus passed away one of the colossal men of the century—a man who rose from the obscurity of a Western pioneer's life to the highest distinction which the intellect can command in the American Republic, and whose noble qualities and honorable name are heritage enough to distinguish those he left behind.

E. B.

FUNERAL CEREMONIES.

From the Lancaster paper.

It had been announced that the funeral ceremonies would commence at eleven o'clock, on Saturday last, at the Catholic church, and previous to that hour citizens and strangers proceeded in large numbers towards the Ewing mansion, so that, before the hour above named, the house, the grounds, and the streets in the immediate vicinity were thronged with people. Every one seemed to appreciate the fact that a great man had passed away, and the manifestations of respect were of that quiet but earnest character that represents sincerity. A long line of people passed through the house to look for the last time on the face of the great statesman. It was remarked by those who had seen Mr. Ewing within a year that emaciation had accomplished more on his countenance than they had anticipated; but the marks of a master-mind could not be effaced, and even in death the countenance reflected greatness.

All of Mr. Ewing's sons and daughters, with their families, were present, including Judge P. B. Ewing, General Hugh Ewing, General Thomas Ewing, General Charles Ewing, General W. T. Sherman, with his wife and family, and Colonel Steele and wife.

At the appointed hour, the procession was formed and moved on foot to St. Mary's Catholic Church, the follow-

ing gentlemen acting as pall-bearers: Messrs. H. H.
Hunter, Michael A. Daugherty, John T. Brazee, John D.
Martin, James R. Pearce, D. Tallmadge, Charles Bor-
land, G. G. Beck, S. A. Griswold, F. A. Foster, Samuel
Herr, C. M. L. Wiseman, Jacob Beck, T. O. Edwards,
and J. F. Vandemark, all of Lancaster; Hon. Henry
Stanbery, of Kentucky; Governor R. B. Hayes, of Ohio;
Hon. A. G. Thurman, of Columbus; Hon. John Sher-
man, of Mansfield; Hon. John Welch, of Athens;
Colonel John H. James, of Urbana; Hon. George Reber,
of Sandusky; Hon. A. B. Walker, of Athens; General
H. B. Curtis, of Mt. Vernon; W. Marshall Anderson, of
Circleville; and C. B. Goddard, of Zanesville.

The auditorium of the church was filled with people,
and the ceremonies were conducted by Rev. Father
Young, formerly of Perry County, one of the oldest
priests in the United States; at their conclusion, Archbishop Purcell, of Cincinnati, delivered an address, in
which he spoke in the highest terms of the character of
the deceased. The Archbishop spoke of Mr. Ewing's
good citizenship, his devotedness as a father, the purity
of his patriotism, and the greatness of his mind. Contemporary with Clay, Webster, Calhoun, and Hayne, he was
worthy of the high rank he took in the counsels of the
nation when such distinguished men were in the field of
statesmanship. He had risen by sterling merit, and was
as much a model in his private relations as he was in his
relations to the country. He was a man who never for-
got a favor, and had frequently made substantial expres-

sions of his gratitude to those who had comforted him or those dear to him in hours of affliction. The Archbishop spoke of Mr. Ewing's relations to the Catholic Church; for thirty-eight years, while practising liberality to the religious opinions of all, he had expressed his conviction that the evidence was in favor of the church with which he finally connected himself during his last illness.

At the conclusion of the address, the procession reformed, and proceeded to the cemetery in carriages, in the following order:

First, pall-bearers; second, hearse; third, the family; fourth, visitors; fifth, members of the bar and city council of Lancaster; sixth, citizens.

At the cemetery, the Catholic ceremonies were observed, and the remains of Mr. Ewing were interred beside those of his wife, who died seven years ago.

Among the strangers present were Judges Welch, White, and McIlvaine, of the Supreme Court of Ohio; Hon. John Sherman and Hon. Allen G. Thurman, United States Senators; Governor R. B. Hayes, General I. R. Sherwood, General F. B. Pond, General W. T. Wilson, Judge John L. Greene, Judge James L. Bates, M. M. Green, Esq., Adjutant-General Knapp, L. J. Critchfield, Esq., Colonel L. Baber, Rev. A. G. Byers, Thomas Miller, Esq., General C. C. Walcutt, R. C. Hoffman, Esq., General H. B. Curtis, of Mt. Vernon, Colonel John H. James, of Urbana, and a number of gentlemen from Logan, including Judges Grogan, Wright, Alfred, and many others.

"Finis coronat Opus."

FAMILY TESTIMONY.

WASHINGTON, D. C., Nov. 14, 1872.

HON. P. B. EWING, LANCASTER, OHIO:

MY DEAR BROTHER: As you are aware, I am arrang-
ing papers for the publication of a memorial of our
beloved father, for distribution among his particular
personal friends, but mainly for preservation among
his own children and grandchildren, and by them to
be handed down to their descendants, in testimony
of the fact that before his death he was blessed with
the fulness of faith—that faith to the intellectual
acknowledgment of which his researches and his
reason had long before brought him, and for the
possession of which his heart had long anxiously
yearned.

I desire also in this way to preserve for his descendants the evidences and expressions of the respect
and veneration, of the affection and honor, in which
he was held by his countrymen. To meet this end,
I shall publish some private communications addressed
to different members of the family after his death;
the newspaper notices of that event and of his funeral;
and the proceedings of public bodies in different cities
of the State and in the Capitol of the nation on the

occasion of his death. These will be grateful testimonials of the noble life of him of whom those who
knew him longest and best could say, "After a long
life of usefulness, he has left us a reputation of pure
moral excellence without a spot or a single blemish."

The greater number of these publications will bear
evidence of the fact that he came into the church.
We, his children, who with loving solicitude so long
watched for the coming of this transcendent gift of
faith, saw his mind and heart for years draw nearer
and more near the truth, until at last the crowning
blessing of his life was given.

Men prejudiced against the church would have
forborne their invidious criticism on the consoling
solemnities of his funeral could they have known,
as we well knew, how he loved and reverenced the
ceremonies and services of the church. Tenderly and
reverently do I recall the days when, unable to go
himself to church, he would sit with his windows
raised, listening, with devotional interest, to the music
of the Mass. The beautiful lilac bush, an old relic
in the yard, was even sacrificed because it obstructed
his view of the church. Associated with the recollection of the walk home from church on Sunday is the
vision of that beneficent face and that head, so grand
and noble, which we could see from the distant side-
walk, and the smile so gentle and sweet with which
he would greet us as we entered, asking with interest about the sermon, and listening with pleasure,

and even avidity, to the prayers we would sometimes read to him. The dearest and most fondly remember-ed smile of love and encouragement was ever given me when often, in the early morning, I would pass his windows and look in, and he knew I was going fasting to receive my Lord and Saviour.

Many a time has he spoken to me on the im-portance of shielding my children from the danger of losing their faith in the Catholic Church. Once he charged me never again to let Tommy visit cer-tain friends who had sneeringly laughed at him for declining to be helped to meat on Friday. "Keep him from such places," he said; "for it is cruel to subject so young a child to the ordeal of seeing that which he holds sacred ridiculed, and he might be tempted to be ashamed of his faith—a thing from which you must guard him until he is older and stronger." These friends were on every other ac-count desirable and valued. Also, he enjoined upon me to be ever firm in withholding my children from the public schools. He even declared his intention to himself prevent their attendance at them. "None of these children shall ever attend one," he said, with great emphasis and determination.

Fifteen years before his death, on the occasion of a visit I made with him to Washington, the wife of a distinguished jurist sought a conversation with me on religion. In telling father about it afterward, I said that she had asked me to renew the subject, and I had refused on account of the manner in which she had spoken of the Blessed Virgin. He was much agitated, and, after some reflection, said, "You should have told her that, as God knew from all eternity that she was to be the Mother of his Son, he must have made and preserved her pure and perfect beyond all others."

Two or three years before his death, a holy Jesuit father, now living in the district (Father Stonestreet), at my request called to speak with father on the subject of religion. When I saw him next, he said to me: "I am old and gray-haired myself, but I sat with reverence before your father, and from his conversation I can only say he is very near the kingdom of heaven." Some time before that, you remember, father said to a dear friend (Sister M. Angela) "that his family could not be more anxious for him to have the faith than he himself was to possess it, and that he prayed for it daily." And in the last few weeks of his life, how feelingly he spoke to us of the great blessing we enjoyed in having been brought up in the faith!

When the end of his earthly course drew nigh, and the eternal day was dawning upon him, the talents and wisdom of the natural mind became illumined by the grace which poured in upon his soul as it beheld the great vision.

Divine truth at last penetrated that mind, so grand in its creation, and so perfect in its cultivation, and the noble heart, with all its longings, was at rest. The sacrament. of extreme unction, which a supernatural grace alone enabled him to compose himself to receive in the midst of agonizing suffering, brought grace to him and consolation to us. After that dread night when he seemed in the agonies of death, and during the respite of days that followed, how we rejoiced when he said to us, what he had said the day before, "that he earnestly desired to receive the sacrament of the Holy Eucharist"! That blessing was granted him. He received the body and blood of our Lord, and, in the words of the venerated Archbishop who broke to him the bread of life, "he received in the fulness of faith and in the holiest and happiest of dispositions."

In our anguish at parting with him who for so long a time had been to us an idol so loving and beloved, so strong and so gentle, so bound up with every thought and feeling of our minds and hearts that to lose him was to lose too much of earth— even in the anguish of that time, the great blessing vouchsafed forced from us the prayer of thanksgiving and joy: "O Lord! thou hast crowned us as with a shield of thy good-will." Up to the moment of his departure hence, our whole lives had been bound to him by all the dear and tender ties of earth; for he had shared our every joy and grief, and his sympathetic heart responded to even the slightest of our interests. Those ties strengthened with every year of his prolonged existence, and grew more and more sacred and tender, until at last it seemed almost impossible to live without him, and terrible to see him die.

The glorious sunset, the magnificently illuminated clouds and sky, which, closing a day of gloom and rain, greeted our eyes as we lifted them to heaven after leaving him dead, typify to my mind and heart the glory of his soul, which had so recently passed through a season of gloom, and suffering, and sorrow.

The blessed hope of a reunion in the home of the redeemed is our infinite consolation. Thanksgiving to God that he gave us so grand and good a father, that he so singularly blest him throughout life, and that he bestowed upon him the faith which will crown him with everlasting joy and glory, will ever continue to be our prayer.

I am your very affectionate sister,

ELLEN EWING SHERMAN.

LANCASTER, OHIO, Nov. 24, 1872.

MRS. E. E. SHERMAN:

MY DEAR SISTER: Your letter was received and read with deep interest and satisfaction. It is a touching monument of filial piety, and will serve admirably as a preface to the memorial volume.

An incident which occurs to me as deserving of place, but which you have omitted, is the familiar fact that for twenty-five years or more he kept close at hand and carried with him in his journeys the Thomas à Kempis so affectionately presented to him by his good friend the Archbishop; and you remember that Viney told us that he was impressed with the assiduity with which he used to read it during the long nights of his last years while he watched with and served him.

From the difference in our relations to him, you cannot know as well as I the mark of grace and predilection that he bore through all his life in the elevation and purity of mind which adorned him, even more than the strength and vigor of intellect for which he was so distinguished.

I went into his office as a student in the fall of 1839, and from that date down to his death, a period of more than thirty years, I was very much with him, in the most intimate and confidential relations, through all the vicissitudes of his political, professional, and social life; and I can say with confidence that never, in my whole life, did I hear from his lips a profane or irreverent word. All that I ever saw or knew of him left the reverent conviction that not his words only, but his very thoughts, might be photographed and read without impeachment of his observance of every known trust or duty, and without confusion in the presence of the purest and best among men.

I specially desire to record my testimony to some

of the interesting events of the last days of our honored father, and gladly avail myself of your offer to make place for it in the memorial. To this end, I give you the enclosed letter, written when these events were just passed, and the scenes and language were fresh in my memory. I also send a copy of my memorandum of an interesting date.

As ever, my dear sister,

Your affectionate brother,

P. B. EWING.

The following is a portion of the letter to which my brother refers, and which was written to Mrs. M. M. Phelan, then at Notre Dame, Ind.:

LANCASTER, OHIO, Nov. 2, 1871.

MY DEAR —— : I have much more to say to you on the subject of the last days of dear father than I can find space for in a single letter.

In all, the grace and good providence of Almighty God were manifested in disposing and preparing his mind and heart for the supreme event, as fruit is ripened and made perfect by the kindly rays of the sun.

You know how, in the early missionary days, his home was always open to the Catholic priests, many of whom were entertained by him for weeks and even months together, and always as most valued friends and welcome guests. For weeks before his death his mind was dwelling on those old times and his association with those early priests; and, while we were corresponding with the Archbishop, and anxiously looking to him as the one whose hands would lead his last steps into the ark, good Father Dominic (almost the sole survivor of those old associates), coming from his distant home, presented himself uninvited and unexpected, but a most welcome visitor. Reaching Lancaster on the 18th, without seeing any one, he went directly to father's room, and, finding him alone, had a long and satisfactory interview with him on the subject of religion. He spent that evening at our house, and said that he was so well assured of father's faith and disposition that, if he were dying, he would have no doubt or hesitation about giving him absolution.

We had just retired for the night, when we were startled by a message to the effect that father had a severe chill; and we were soon assembled to find him in a fever, and in such distress that he constantly rose to his feet, and, supporting himself for a moment with assistance, sank to his chair to rise again the next minute, and unable or unwilling to take the medicine prescribed for the emergency.

Father Dominic addressed him a few words, telling him to prepare his mind and heart by acts of faith and contrition, while he gave him absolution; and, *receiving his assent*, this was done. Then, say-

ing a few words about extreme unction, he proceeded
to the administration of that sacrament also.   During this time, father remained quietly seated in his
chair, reverential and devout. After some prayers,
Father Dominic left him, as he had grown easier, and
it was probable that he would survive the night.

The next day, Father Dominic visited him, and,
among other things, he said to him, in my presence
and that of other members of the family: " I would
be glad to administer to you the Blessed Sacrament,
if you were now able to receive it," to which he
responded: " I desire it, I ardently desire it; but I
am not now able." (*Father meant that he was not
able to make the full and minute confession which
he thought must precede the reception of the Holy
Eucharist.—E. E. S.*)   The day after, Father Dominic
hoped to find him in better condition, but it was
still deferred; and the Archbishop came in the evening, but he did not see father until the following day,
which was Saturday. Then, taking the Host in his
hands, the Archbishop, accompanied by Father Dominic, came to his bedside, and, in a touching and
effective manner, prepared him for the crowning glory
of his life, and administered the holy viaticum;
received by him, in the language of the Archbishop,
" in the fulness of the faith, and with marks of the
utmost reverence and devotion."

I cannot express the feelings of my heart at this
solemn and affecting hour. You know how my

father was beloved and venerated, and how he was more than worthy of all the love and veneration that my poor heart can hold.

Below I give extracts from the memorandum:

Oct. 19, 1871.—"About ten o'clock this morning, father called me to his side (Hugh and Maria being also present), and said: 'I wish you to pay out of my estate a gift *donatis causa mortis* of one thousand dollars to the Catholic clergy of the diocese of Cincinnati, in recognition of their valuable and appreciated aid, by counsel, instruction, and example, in the right education and rearing of my children. I hardly know how to designate the proper beneficiaries of this gift; but you may place it in the hands of Archbishop Purcell, to be disposed of at his good discretion.'"

(*This was the only bequest that father made in contemplation of death, except that he made provision for an annuity, in the hands of Philemon, for a servant who had been faithful through years; later in the day, when giving some further instructions, he suggested that his horses and carriage should be given to the members of the family in whose care and use they then were.—E. E. S.*)

"At a few minutes before six P.M., father again called me, and said : 'I wish to give you some directions as to my funeral. I cannot expect to survive more than a few days, perhaps a week, may be not twenty-four hours. I wish that my funeral be plain and simple; that I be buried by the side of your mother, and have a monument over my grave like hers in design, but larger and with suitable inscriptions.' After a pause, he said, 'I think I leave my family and affairs in good condition.' To this I made some suitable reply. After some interval, he said: 'And then, Ellen should not lament for me. I have been already spared to my family for a term long exceeding that that belongs to humanity, though she will no doubt feel my loss more than if I had died twenty years ago.'

"After some period of reflection, with tears coming to his eyes, he fell off into a doze, on rousing from which he was assisted to the bed.

P. B. EWING.

"P.S.—He never rose from his bed again.

P. B. E."

in pinen

1863

Sacred

To the memory of
Maria Ewing
Who was born Jany 1st 1801
Was married Jany 7th 1820
And died Febry 20th 1864

Mulierum amantissima—
Requiescat in pace

She had Sympathy and Solace
for those in Misfortune
Was
Charitable to the Poor,

In her own household
a pattern of domestic virtue;
Her Children
have risen up and called her
blessed.

WASHINGTON, D. C., May 20, 1873.

MY DEAR SISTER: I give below some extracts from my journal relating to father's formal reception into the church. All the evidence that came to my attention in his conversation and action since the year 1851, of his belief in and love and reverence for the church, would fill a volume. His delay in entering the visible church was due alone to scrupulosity; fear of the opinion of the world had no share in it, for it is well known that he took pleasure in braving that opinion when it ran counter to truth. Shortly after my return from Europe, some one in our presence opposed the doctrine of the infallibility of the Pope; when father said: "It is a logical necessity, and the trouble is not in believing, but in disbelieving it." His familiarity with sacred history and the writings of eminent churchmen was begun early and continued through life. When driving out one day (Oct. 5, 1853), he said to me: "When I was six years old—that is, in my sixth winter—I read the Bible through from beginning to end. I was so young that I thought the four Gospels related to four different advents of Christ; and I was much disappointed when, on asking father, he told me that they all referred to the same advent." Below are my later extracts.

Your loving brother,

HUGH EWING.

8

Extracts.

Oct. 16, Monday.—He said in the evening to me: "The young man is fortunate and happy who has Catholic faith, it is so firm and living. He may err, but, if his faith remain unshaken, he will come back. The priests of the church alone can guide young men."

19th, Thursday.—Father has had a chill; in great distress. Father Dominic gave him absolution and extreme unction, and said prayers, in which we all joined. He consented to and received the sacrament with great quiet and attention, suppressing his previous and after-movements, as rising, etc. This afternoon, Father Dominic had another interview. Father responded firmly and decidedly that he was sorry for his sins; that he had full and entire faith in all the articles of faith; and, in response to Father Dominic's remark that he wished he could receive holy communion, he said: "I wish I could, I earnestly desire to do so."

21st, Saturday.—At 3.20 P.M. the Archbishop came over, dressed in his cassock, cross, etc., with the Blessed Sacrament; told father he had brought him the crowning blessing of his life—the body and blood, soul and divinity, of Jesus Christ; that, in his condition, he would not require confession; asked if he had a hearty sorrow for all the sins of his life, a firm faith in the church, and hope in the Redeemer, and

love of God. He answered, "I can truly say I have."
He then received absolution and Holy Communion
with all the reverence and devotion of one brought
up in the church. "I never saw any one in my
life receive with more evidences of devotion" (Archbishop). The Archbishop then advised and prayed with
him. Father Dominic and Rose present, others kneeling outside. He has been serene and happy since.

26th, Thursday.—Father died at ten minutes before
four o'clock this afternoon, after receiving the last
benediction, so calmly that for some minutes it was
not perceptible. A beautiful sunset.

LANCASTER, OHIO, June 28, 1873.

DEAR ——: Yours of 24th inst. is at hand. I will-
ingly unite my evidence with that of others who
had the same opportunity of knowing that your good
father died a Christian death and a sincere member
of the Catholic Church.

The Saturday preceding his death, and before the
visit of Archbishop Purcell, who gave him the sacrament,
I was alone in attendance on him for some time. He
was restless and anxious in his manner, and seemed
uncomfortable and unhappy. He complained of no
pain, but could not rest, and I could do nothing to
relieve him. After observing him closely for awhile, I
became satisfied he wanted to see *some one*, and I

was equally satisfied, for different reasons, that the person he wanted was the Priest. I left the room to ask some one to send for him, and at the hall door I met Philemon, and told him what I thought. He said that Archbishop Purcell had arrived, and he would bring him over at once, which he did. When I returned to your father's bedside after the Archbishop had given him the sacrament, I was struck with the change. He lay quiet and peaceful, nothing but calm contentment in his expression. I proposed after awhile that he should try and sleep, and arranged the pillows for him. He smiled and made some kind remark, then sank into a quiet sleep of over two hours. I know how much importance you attach to your own form of faith, and I have often wished that you, his children, could have seen as I did how full of belief he was, and how much comfort it gave him to be received into your communion. I can never forget that day any more than I can forget him and all his goodness.

Affectionately,

C. STEELE.

_____

LANCASTER, OHIO, May 17, 1873.

MY DEAR SISTER : I enclose for the purposes of your memorial a lengthy extract from a letter to a friend, in which I have detailed the circumstances attending the last days of our beloved father, especially those relating

to his reception in faith and love of the adorable Sacrament of the Eucharist.

Ever your affectionate sister,

MARIA EWING STEELE.

When Father Dominic suggested to him on Friday
to make his confession in preparation for receiving the
Blessed Eucharist, he was suffering from great pain and
exhaustion, and said he was not able to "commence it."
When, however, the Archbishop arrived on Saturday, he
went to father's room carrying with him the holy viaticum.   Father evinced the greatest comfort and consolation at seeing the Archbishop, who, approaching his bedside, said, "Mr. Ewing, I have come to bring you the
crowning blessing of your life—the body and blood of
your divine Redeemer.   I know that you are now too ill
to make a regular confession, but, if you can say to me in
sincerity and truth that you believe in all the doctrines
of the Holy Catholic Church, and that you repent of
all the sins of your past life, and beg pardon of God
for them—say this to me in God's holy presence, and
that is all that will be necessary in your feeble state
before giving you the bread of life."   Father responded
fervently and solemnly, "All that I can say from the
bottom of my heart, and I will be most thankful to receive
from you the holy Host."   During the entire day preceding the Archbishop's visit, which was late in the
afternoon, the Colonel, who was watching with father,

was distressed by his restlessness and disquiet, which
was more mental than physical, anxious evidently for
the presence of some one; for, when questioned as to his
physical wants, there was nothing he wished done for
him. But from the moment of the Archbishop's visit,
and the reception of the Sacrament, he was in a state
of perfect calm and quiet, and after a time sank into a
sweet and restful sleep that seemed so like the sleep of
health and ease that we found our longing hearts hoping that a respite would be granted, and that dear and
gentle life prolonged yet a little while. But "his eyes
had seen his salvation, and he was ready to depart in
peace." ⅼ

--- --- --- --- ---

HEADQUARTERS ARMY OF THE UNITED STATES, }
WASHINGTON, D. C., July 15, 1873.   }

DEAREST ELLEN : General Hugh Ewing has requested
me to contribute a letter for the personal memorial of
your father, the Hon. Thomas Ewing, which you are
preparing for publication. I find it difficult to write
anything concise and short that approaches justice to the
subject. I cannot well separate your father's memory
from public events, when manifesting my sense of gratitude and praise of him, and simple eulogy sounds bare
when speaking of an historic character. Hugh asked
me to allude to the fact that your father died in the
Catholic Church. It struck me as something out of my
line entirely; for the fact was evidenced at the time,

and needs no confirmation from me. With that event others can deal fully, truthfully, and naturally, but it would sit awkwardly on my pen.

His life extending from 1789 to 1871, through probably the most active period of the world's history, beginning when Ohio was a wilderness, sharing in the labor of clearing her forests, opening her mines, and establishing the schools and colleges that now adorn her, then transferred to a higher sphere, and sharing in the politics and government of a great nation, his biography assumes the rank of history. In the world at large the fame of Thomas Ewing was secure when transferred from Ohio to the United States Senate; he at once took first rank among the statesmen of that most brilliant period, and was second to none as a lawyer before the Supreme Court of the United States. Whoever assumes the task of biographer must show how, by industry well directed, he had gathered his immense fund of facts, arranged them in logical order, clothed them in pure language, and announced them with that earnestness and force which characterized his speeches and writings. We, however, who enjoyed a more intimate relation, can recall his natural love for the good and beautiful; how he would recite from Homer and Virgil, from Addison and Scott, with innumerable pieces of fugitive poetry that from time to time attracted his notice, but never escaped his memory. We recall also his knowledge of pure mathematics, and how utterly impossible it was to impose on him by partial or imperfect demonstration, and how quickly he would detect any explanation of an event not consistent with pure truth and logic.

My personal recollections of him date back to a very early period, when I was a mere child and he a man in full career of life.

On my way to West Point, in 1836, by his direction I came to Washington, where he was at the time a Senator from Ohio. I found him boarding with Mrs. Hill, who had a son at West Point. The mess of which he was a member consisted of some of the most brilliant men of the day, and I now recall their wit and humor, in which he always led off, and which was in marked contrast to the bitter political wrangles that prevailed then in Congress and in the press. One day, in walking along Pennsylvania Avenue, we overtook Hon. Samuel L. Southard, to whom he introduced me as his young ward *en route* to West Point. Mr. Southard said, "Young man, I can only say to you, as I used to say to others when I was Secretary of the Navy, be industrious and obedient, and you have nothing to fear."

I was in correspondence with Mr. Ewing throughout the Civil war. He took the most intense interest in every event, and at almost every stage of its existence he wrote encouraging me to the boldest action, yet looking to the success of our arms and cause without imperilling the principles of the Government itself, in which he had the full faith he had in natural law. To him extreme measures were only justified to produce peace, and that peace should leave the National and

State Governments, with all their rights and limits as defined by the Constitution, unimpaired and unchanged. As the war approached its conclusion, I could see from the tone of his letters his fears and apprehensions on this point, and that the success of arms might give a bias to the people at large, and so increase the power of the National Government as to take from the State and local governments the ability to manage successfully the matters that should rightfully be left to them. In dealing with the last stage of his public career, none but a great constitutional lawyer can do justice to his memory, and therefore I trust that will fall into competent hands.

In private life, he was eminently social, full of humor and wit, and encouraging enterprise on the part of the young. To all connected with him he was full of sympathy, and gave assistance and advice to all who applied. As an example to others, your father's memoir will be almost a perfect model, and, as a part of history, his own is an epitome of that of the country itself.

Affectionately,

W. T. SHERMAN,

General.

WASHINGTON, D. C., 11th June, 1873.

MY DEAR SISTER: Having read with great interest Mr. Huntington's account of his journey from the faith in which he had been educated, through the dif-

ferent Christian denominations, in which he paused for
a time, to the Catholic Church, where his soul found
the food and rest it was seeking, I spoke of it to
father, and he directed me to leave it on his table
that he might read it. A day or two after, he returned the book to me, saying that he was much
pleased with it, but that the author had omitted a
very strong argument in favor of the church that he
should have given, which he then stated at some
length. I was so much impressed with this conversation that I requested father to give me the sub-
stance of it in writing, saying that I wished to preserve it; for I wanted to keep, in his own hand and
language, the tribute of respect which he had paid
to the devotions the church has established in honor of the Blessed Virgin. The following day, he
handed me a letter dated the 3d of May, 1870, giving in brief the proposition he had laid down and
discussed the day before, *i.e.*, that "we owe to the
Catholic Church the institution of families and the
elevated social condition of woman." I now give this
letter to you as my contribution to the memorial you
are preparing to perpetuate the memory of his virtuous
life and the blessing that crowned its close.

Through life I have gathered father's opinions on
religious questions solely from expressions that current events called out. In all these, my memory
from my earliest childhood to the last day of his
life records no word or act of his in disparagement of

the church or her dogmas. He often had for her
words of praise, but never one of censure. Those
who have been of his household have ever heard
him speak in commendation of her great wisdom,
her teachings, her practices, and her priests.

Of the incidents of father's last days there is but
little that I can give you except what you already
have from other members of the family; but there is
one event of which I should speak, although others
will doubtless give it. During the last ten days of
his life, I watched at his bedside and served him
with an anxious heart, though my hands were un-
skilful and my service of little value; and it chanced
that a servant and I were alone with him for a
short time in the afternoon of the 21st of October,
when Archbishop Purcell entered his room bearing
with him the Holy Eucharist. I could not be present
at the confession which I knew must precede the
reception of this sacrament, and I therefore went out
and stood near by, where I was within call, and
could hear the murmur of voices in the room, but
could not distinguish words. After a short time had
elapsed, I heard the Archbishop, in a distinct tone
of voice, pronouncing absolution, when I summoned
Philemon and other members of the family from an
adjoining room where they were waiting, and, going
with them to the door of father's room, and kneeling,
we heard the Archbishop pronouncing the usual
formula, "The body of our Lord Jesus Christ pre-

serve thy soul unto life everlasting," as father received
the Blessed Sacrament—the long hoped-for, prayed-for
blessing that mother taught us in infancy to ask.

I cannot refrain from giving you another incident
which has since become doubly dear to me, and will
show how his kind heart always went out to his
children, as he thought of us and of our children
even to the last. It was late in the afternoon of the
25th of October, the day before he died, as I sat by
his bedside holding his pale hand in both of mine,
and, looking into his face, thought that he was sleeping, that he said to me, "How is my little friend?"
I was half persuaded that he was dreaming. Still, I
asked him what he meant, when he turned his eyes
upon me, and said, "How is my little friend in Washington?" He was thinking of his youngest grandchild,
my little Lizzie, who had not half as many days of
life as he had years. I answered that she was
"flourishing," when he said, "Not like the green bay-
tree, for she is young and innocent." She was innocent and pure, and will ever be; for, although she
was the last concerning whom he asked on earth,
she was the first to follow him to heaven. Father
had no favorite child. Through his long life his
solicitude was strong, and he was ever watchful
and wise in his care for all of us; from Philemon
to my little daughter, the first and last of his children, all were embraced in his thoughtful care even
to the last day of his life.

As father's advice determined the question as to
the kind of material to be used in building the main
altar in our church at Lancaster, it may not be out
of place for me to record here the interest he took
in the matter when it was first under discussion. It
had been suggested that the altar should be built,
not of wood or marble, as was the custom in our
churches, but of the rich brown sandstone from the
quarries near Lancaster. It was urged that, when
an altar was raised from which to offer the solemn
sacrifice of the Mass, it should be built of the rock
that nature furnished to the hand of the builder;
and that a massive altar richer in ornamentation
could be built of our sandstone than we could pos-
sibly make of wood or marble. This suggestion did
not meet with favor from any one until it was presented to father. He approved it warmly, and said
that he would give for this purpose the "Chestnut-
tree rock" on his farm—a huge square block of stone
that had in a remote age been torn from its place in
the ridge beyond by some giant force in nature, and
placed altar-like on the crest of a hill that stood out
from its neighbors, and overlooked the valley for miles
on either hand; and he said that doubtless it had
been set apart from the ledge more years than he
could tell to harden and bleach for this purpose.
This was years before we, his children, thought to
raise this altar to the honor of God and to the memory
of father and mother; but now that they have gone

to rest with the benediction of the church, this majestic altar—its table, broad and deep, of solid rock, on which six monolithic pillars rest, supporting the rich cornice and canopy of stone that overhangs the place of sacrifice, and bearing on its front in letters of bronze the dedication, "Gloria Dei"—will be built by his children from the rock that father gave, and it will for generations yet to come be an altar of sacrifice, and, speaking from the past, it will perpetuate, among the descendants of those who knew and honored them in this life, the virtues of two of God's servants who through life obeyed his law.

I am, my dear sister,

Your loving brother,

CHARLES EWING.

To MRS. ELLEN EWING SHERMAN,

WASHINGTON, D. C.

" *The unanimous praise of the good, the unbought voice of those who can well discriminate as to surpassing virtue.*"

LETTERS AND TELEGRAMS FROM FRIENDS.

CINCINNATI, Oct. 24, 1871.

DEAR GENERAL: I have just received yours of the 23d. I must go to Columbus to-morrow to argue before the Supreme Court the constitutionality of the law authorizing Cincinnati to subscribe $10,000,000 to the Southern Railway—an engagement I cannot postpone or forego. No private business or ordinary professional engagement would prevent my going to Lancaster at once. So soon as that imperative duty is performed, I will hasten to Lancaster in the hope of once more seeing your father in life, or, if too late for that, at least to pay the last tribute of affection and respect to him, my guide and friend through all my professional life.

Sincerely yours,

HENRY STANBERY.

GENL. THOS. EWING, JR.

ATHENS, OHIO, Oct. 27, 1871.

DEAR SIR: Your telegram, freighted with the sad intelligence of the death of Mr. Ewing, Ohio's noblest son, was duly received and the message passed round among his numerous friends last evening as far as prac-

10

ticable.   This morning, our citizens are all advised of
this public bereavement, and our place will be numer-
ously represented at the funeral to-morrow.

Among others, I called on General Brown and Judge
A. G. Brown last evening.   The General will not be
able to go up to the funeral, but he spoke of Mr. Ewing's
age, that, if he had been spared till the 28th of next
December, he would have completed his 82d year, and
of his own age, that on the first of the same month
he will be 86.   They were attached friends throughout
their lives, and among the noblest specimens of humanity
that we have known.

I have an autograph letter of his of August 30, 1871,
which will be preserved most sacredly as a precious relic
of the great man, so long and favorably known, and
whom I could not doubt was ever my sincere friend.
Our entire community will sympathize with yours and
the bereaved family on this occasion.

Respectfully,

A. B. WALKER.

HON. H. II. HUNTER.

QUINCY, ILLINOIS, Oct. 27, 1871.

MY DEAR GENERAL: Your telegram announcing the
death of our distinguished friend, Hon. Thomas Ewing,
reached me, in the night, last night.   Accept my thanks
for your kind attention.

I am not surprised, but grieved.   I had hoped to see

him once more before he passed beyond the boundary of time; but he is gone, and the hope cannot now be realized. His was a long, useful, honorable, and eminent career; and I am proud to claim him as my countryman and friend. He was, I believe, the last of the great senators who shed so much lustre upon our country in the first half of the present century.

He leaves behind him, in all the land, no one combining so much of patriotism, learning, wisdom, and experience. He was a very remarkable man, and a great and good one. His name now passes proudly into history, and will live there as long as love of just and good government, and admiration of great and good qualities of our kind, endure.

It occasions me sincere regret that I cannot show my veneration for his character by being present at his funeral; but court is in session here, and I am tied down to the trial of important cases, from which I cannot escape.

Mrs. Browning and Emma unite with me in kind regards and sympathy for all.

Most truly your friend,

O. H. BROWNING.

GENERAL W. T. SHERMAN,
  Lancaster, Ohio.

AUGUSTA, MAINE, SUNDAY, NOV. 5, 1871.

MY DEAR COUSIN: I hardly feel that you can expect or desire letters of condolence on the death of your father.   Such a death after such a life is not matter of grief, but of joy.   To what a small number of the hundreds of millions of the human race is so much given as was given to your father! By what a small number is so much done!

He was a grand and massive man, almost without peers. With no little familiarity and association with the leading men of the day, I can truly say that I never met one who impressed me so profoundly.

'   His memory is a heritage to all his descendants of the most precious and inestimable type. . . .

Affectionately your cousin,

J. G. BLAINE.

To Mrs. ELLEN B. E. SHERMAN.

———————

PARIS, Nov. 20, 1871.

DEAR MRS. SHERMAN: Across the wide ocean comes to my ears the sad news that another light has gone out, that another great man has fallen; and to me, more than all else, that one who was to me a second father sleeps at last beside her who fulfilled every day of her life a saint's mission, and who ever reaps, I doubt not, a saint's reward.

Ever known for his incorruptible integrity; a giant in intellect in the days when there were giants in the land; possessing in a most marked degree the respect and love of all who knew him—at last, full of years, he has yielded to a power that none can mock, and the places that have so long known him shall know him no more for ever. Had I been in the United States, nothing would have prevented me from being a humble but sincere mourner among those who followed him to his last resting-place.

I need not say to you how deeply I sympathize with you in this sad hour; for I knew him as comparatively few knew him—at home, in the bosom of his family, in that sacred spot where men throw off the mask they are too often compelled to wear in their intercourse with the world; and, thus knowing him, I know your loss.

But as I read of the general expression of sympathy which has gone up from all parts of the country; of the universal testimony from bench and bar, and from politicians of all parties, as to his acknowledged ability and spotless life, I am consoled, and take courage for the future of my country—a country which, though too often bowing the knee to the golden calf, and elevating to positions of trust and honor men of no intellect and of no honesty, at last over an open grave is able to distinguish between merit and charletanism, between tinsel and pure gold. It is a hopeful sign, and goes far to redeem its many shortcomings.

Ever and sincerely your friend,

William Slade.

Buffalo, Oct. 31, 1871.

Mrs. General Sherman :

Dear Madam : I trust you will pardon the liberty I

take in expressing my sympathy in this your hour of deep affliction. 'Tis said "the sympathy of friends in affliction charms away half the woe." If so, I know you will find the cup less bitter; for your friends are Legion, and your trust is in God.

To me the memory of your dear father was like a beacon-light; for away back in my early youth, a kind and affectionate father taught me to love and honor the man who was his youthful companion in the early hardships of a Western life, viz., Thomas Ewing, and whom in my manhood I was moved to admire and cherish.

I shall never forget the numerous kind letters found among my father's correspondence, written in early life by your noble father, some of which I believe one of my brothers has.

But I dare not trespass longer on your kindness. Accept, dear madam, my condolence, and believe me when I tell you that we all deeply sympathize with you and yours in this great bereavement. Kind regards to the General.

Very truly your obedient,

S. S. GUTHRIE.

From the Archbishop of San Francisco.

SAN FRANCISCO, Dec. 3, 1871.

DEAR IN CHRIST, MRS. SHERMAN: I do not send you my condolence, but my joy. Death, it is true, brings on sadness, especially the death of our parents. At your

father's death, your tears were no doubt accompanied
with heavenly joy.

It was only to-day, having just returned from blessing
the first Catholic church in Utah Territory, that I learned the fact of your father's entering the ark, the bosom
of his mother.   God has heard your long and earnest
prayer.   I believe I also prayed for that ever since 1841,
when your dear mother gave me the finest room in her
house.   I have been filled with joy at the reading of
your father receiving the Holy Sacraments.

Well, let us return thanks to God, and let us pray
that not only the statesmen, but also the generals, may
join the choir, and sing the Catholic creed—the only
one made by the apostles and taught by Christ.

When I was in Washington last, I wished very much
to call and see you; but I arrived there late in the evening, and had to leave the same evening for Rome.

Please to give my kind regards to the General, and my
best wishes to all your family.

Very respectfully,

JOSEPH S. ALEMANY.

MRS. E. SHERMAN, ETC.

SWANTON, VERMONT, Nov. 3, 1871.

MY DEAR MRS. SHERMAN: I feel assured you will
pardon me for yielding to the impulse which urged me,
as I this moment read the notice of the departure of
your thrice-honored father, in the *Journal* of to-day, to

offer you my most sincere and heartfelt sympathy for a loss in which the nation mourns with you.

With expressions of sympathy I must also join fervent congratulations that he was permitted to seal the record of a noble and illustrious life by the closing act, which opened the golden gates of the glorious city of God to him as he passed to his reward.

I have not failed to comply daily with your parting injunction to me at St. Albans; and the fervor of my poor prayers was redoubled when I saw notices of the alarming state of his health. Joy and thanksgiving mingle with regretful sorrow over an event which has removed one of the few remaining monuments of our former national glory.

May God raise up others like him and his distinguished compeers to rescue our dear country from impending perils, and shed new lustre upon the new Union, bathed with a nation's tears, and cemented with a nation's blood!

Accept, dear Mrs. Sherman, for yourself and family, assurances of our distinguished regard and deep sympathy.

Very truly and sincerely yours,

JULIA C. SMALLEY.

The following is from Judge Samuel Reber.

ST. LOUIS, Oct. 30, 1871.

MY DEAR GENERAL: Your favor of the 13th was duly

received, and I would have answered it sooner, but I
learned through the newspapers that you had gone to
Ohio, to watch the last struggles of a mighty spirit with
that destiny which ultimately overcomes the bravest and
strongest.   Mr. Ewing fell full of years and full of
honors—honors achieved by an intellect almost peerless
among his countrymen.   He was one of the giants of the
last age who have lived into our time.   Who can wield
the sword or wear the armor of the departed hero?

We do not mourn his death immoderately, for *that* is
the lot of all men; but we do lament that so much greatness, so much learning, and so much of the wisdom of
experience cannot be transmitted to others; that it must
all be buried in the grave.   " How inexorable is
death!"   His memory will live!   And may the green
turf rest lightly upon his grave!   .   .   .

Dr. N. Harris to Judge Philemon B. Ewing.

SPRINGFIELD, ILLINOIS, Feb. 21, 1872.

HONORED AND DEAR SIR: Just before your dear and
honored father died, I received a paper from Cincinnati
giving me the first notice of his illness; but I was not
able to visit him, and his death soon after made it impossible to tender to him in person my sincere and
hearty thanks for his great kindness to me for so many
years.   A friend and relative, I am happy to say,
occupied a warm place in my affections that no other
man has ever occupied.   I am glad my dear old friend

11

and cousin was buried in the Catholic faith.   You may
remember that I was always a liberal Presbyterian; and,
as my mother, Sarah Carroll, was a Catholic, I hope to
meet her and a good many of my Catholic friends who
have been so kind to me in that good world where sin
will never come.   .   .   .

I was much disappointed with the history of your
grandfather, Captain George Ewing.   He did not sell his
farm on credit, but for $8,000 cash, and loaned it to the
Government, and, after six years and a half in the army,
he returned, to find his estate all gone, and, like my
mother, received Continental pictures, not worth five
cents on the dollar.   He was a noble man, a good officer,
and was much respected.

If Mrs. Sherman has not, please send me a likeness of
your dear mother.   _____

BROWN UNIVERSITY,
PROVIDENCE, R. I., Oct. 27, 1871.

GEN. THOMAS EWING:

MY DEAR SIR: From a brief reference to your father's
health which fell under my notice a few days since, I
was led to fear that his condition was very critical.   By
a telegram in my morning paper, I see that he breathed
his last in the afternoon of yesterday.   I cannot let this
event, so deeply interesting to the public as well as to
his own bereaved family, pass without offering to you my
sincere sympathy in so great a bereavement.   It was my
good fortune to form the personal acquaintance of your

father some fifteen or twenty years ago. Since that time, I have often met him, and on two or three occasions have been with him for days together.

I have known a goodly number of our eminent statesmen. If I except Daniel Webster, I know not another who has left on my mind so deep an impression of intellectual power and range of knowledge. He never failed to pour a flood of light upon every subject which might chance to fall under discussion, and hence the attractiveness and charm of his conversation. I cannot but feel in his death a sense of personal loss.

In this hour of sorrow, you may well find consolation in his estimable character, his eminent public services, and in the universal respect that will be felt for his memory. More than this, I trust we may all find consolation in the hope that, through the merits of Christ our Saviour, he has entered into the peace and blessedness of them that love God.

Believe me, most sincerely yours,

ALEXIS CASWELL.

CINCINNATI, Oct. 28, 1871.

GEN. THOMAS EWING:

DEAR SIR: Yesterday afternoon, in Indiana, I learned from Cincinnati papers the death of your father. On arriving home, I find a despatch from Mr. Hunter, dated the 26th, announcing it, and learn that my son-in-law, M. Jenney, had forwarded the news, but it had missed me. I was at Richmond attending a family meeting consequent upon the death of Mrs. Perry's mother, who died last Sunday in her seventy-ninth year.

I was well informed of the leading events of your father's life and career preceding the late civil war. Since the opening of the war, I have watched his public expressions, but they have been comparatively few. That his opinions and views have been all the time open, energetic, and decided, no one who knew his constitution could doubt; but my means of knowing them have been less continuous and authentic than before. I have taken it for granted that the part borne in the great struggle by his sons and by Gen. Sherman was such as he would have chosen; and I know from himself that he felt in all its just depths the special personal gratification in their services, which, in a less special form, but not in any less genuine sense, was felt by the whole country. I am glad he lived to see the struggle ended, and to witness the honors of his family. While I do not doubt the coming grandeur and prosperity of our country, public affairs are passing through a stage which it were no great loss to miss. The course of nature having required a great man's eyes to be closed, they are, as to public affairs, closed upon little which he would have cared to see.

At a critical period of your father's political fortunes, I had reason to believe myself in his confidence, and had with him free conferences. The thing which most thrusts itself upon my thoughts at this moment is that I never heard him utter or hint an unmanly or unfair thought.

If he ever sought or wished an unfair advantage in any struggle, I did not suspect it. I look upon him as one of the greatest men I have ever seen. The tendency of my estimate is to place him a little higher, and rank him in a class by himself. Be kind enough to accept for yourself, and to make known to such of your family as would value it, my most sincere and respectful sympathy.

Very truly yours,

AARON F. PERRY.

COLUMBUS, O., Oct. 26, 1871.

To H. H. HUNTER:

The funeral of Mr. Ewing will be attended by myself and other State officers. The Supreme Court will hold no session Saturday, to enable members of the court and bar to attend.   R. B. HAYES.

AUGUSTA, ME., Oct. 27, 1871.

GEN. W. T. SHERMAN:

Just heard of Mr. Ewing's death. I greatly regret that I cannot be present at the funeral ceremonies of one for whom I have all my life cherished the profoundest respect and regard. Mrs. Blaine joins me in expressions of fullest sympathy to the family.

J. G. BLAINE.

WASHINGTON, D. C., Oct. 27, 1871.

GEN. W. T. SHERMAN:

No event could have more profoundly affected the

court and bar than the death of Mr. Ewing. It adds to my own sorrow that I cannot join in his funeral train.

J. M. CARLISLE.

QUINCY, ILL., Oct. 27, 1871.

GEN. W. T. SHERMAN:

Received your telegram last night, and greatly regret that I cannot come to Lancaster. I write you by mail to-day.   O. H. BROWNING

NEW YORK, Oct. 27, 1871.

GEN. AND MRS. SHERMAN:

Most sincerely we sympathize with you in the great loss to the family and the country.

EUGENE CASSERLY,
TERESA CASSERLY,
St. James Hotel.

FROM THE NEWSPAPERS OF THE DAY.

[From the Gazette, Lancaster, Ohio, Thursday, Nov. 2, 1871.]

ON Thursday last, the 26th of October, 1871, at
a quarter to four o'clock in the afternoon, the distinguished citizen of Lancaster, and eminent American statesman, Thomas Ewing, departed this life, in the 82d year
of his age. The state of his health for several months
had prepared all for the solemn event; and when the
final summons came, it found him also prepared. Full
of years and of honors, the cynosure of a nation's
mournful interest, he has passed away, the last, we believe, of that grand array of giant intellects which illuminated the American Senate in the days of Webster,
Clay, Calhoun, Benton, and their contemporaries, who
gave that body the highest distinction it has ever gained.
His last hours were consoled by the presence of his
children and children's children, and of the spiritual
guides whose ministrations were sought in the final
closing of earthly scenes.

The death of no public man of this country could have
created a more profound sensation, or called forth more
general and earnest expressions of sorrow and sympathy.
From the several departments of the national service at
Washington to the smallest municipal organizations, including State Legislatures, judicial bodies, City Coun-

cils, associations of the legal profession, and learned and dignified societies too numerous to name, all have taken formal action to testify their respect for the memory of a great man whose career discloses no blemish to dim its lustre, no public act that can be recalled with regret, no impulse that was not for his country's welfare.

The mass of matter which this event has drawn out from various sources, and of which we have liberally availed ourselves for our columns this week, has left us no space for further remark, even had we the ability to add in the slightest degree to the interest and force of what has been so well said by those whose position as lifelong neighbors and friends enables them so much more fitly to deal with the subject. We need not commend this matter to the attention of our readers, all of whom have felt a noble pride in the great citizen whose loss is now so deeply and widely mourned, which will impart an interest to what we present to-day on this memorable subject that could be supplied by matter of no other character whatever.

———

[Cincinnati Enquirer.]

The telegraph brings the intelligence that Hon. Thomas Ewing is lying at the point of death at his home in Lancaster. Before this paper reaches many of our subscribers, the grave, perhaps, will have closed over the venerable statesman and jurist whose name has been so familiar for the last forty years in the political and judicial annals of Ohio. A sketch of his life and services will be read with interest at this time.

The place of Mr. Ewing's nativity was Ohio County, Virginia. He was born on the 28th day of December, 1789, and is consequently in the 82d year of his age at this time. His father, a man of some means, became considerably reduced during the progress of the Revolutionary war, in which he took a part. After the establishment of peace, the paternal Ewing removed his family to the valley of the Muskingum, in Ohio, and in 1792 he repaired to a frontier settlement, now known as Athens County. It was in this wild region that young Thomas spent his boyhood, and it is quite probable that the rough experiences of a frontier life aroused and developed that fortitude and self-reliance which were such distinguishing elements in his character in after-life. He was taught to read by an elder sister, and gave early indications of remarkable intellectual activity. He read eagerly all the books that came within his reach, pursuing his researches at night by the glowing light of hickory-bark, or the inevitable pine-knot, unfailing resources of light to our ancestors, and always at hand. Having attained his twentieth year, he left the paternal roof, and set out for the Kanawha salt mines to work on his own account. In the course of two or three years, by the exercise of prudence and economy, he saved enough from his scanty earnings to purchase a farm for his father, and with the meagre surplus he entered the Ohio University, and pursued his studies energetically, with occasional interruptions in consequence of failing funds, until the year 1815, when he graduated, receiving the first degree of A.B. ever issued by that educational institution.

Having previously determined to adopt the profession of the law as a means of livelihood, he immediately commenced his studies at Lancaster, Ohio, and was admitted to practice in 1816. From the first his efforts were crowned with success, and he rapidly achieved wealth and reputation, much of his practice in the Supreme Court of the United States being of a remunerative character.

About this time he began to take an active part in politics, and in 1831 he was elected to the United States Senate as a Whig, and became the friend and colleague of Clay and Webster.

He took a prominent and leading position in the Senate, and assailed the Administration for its apparent encroachments. He took strong grounds against the confirmation of Martin Van Buren, who had been designated by the President as Minister to the court of St. James, and was a warm adherent and supporter of the protective-tariff views of Henry Clay. He also lent his influence to the enactment of a law reducing the rates of postage. Among other important measures which he supported was the rechartering of the United States Bank and the revenue collection bill known as the Force Bill. He took an active part in all measures that came before the Senate. As a member of the Committee on Post-Offices and Post-roads, he presented a majority report on

the abuses in the Post-Office Department accompanied by
fourteen resolutions of censure. These resolutions were
subsequently reduced to four, and passed by a small majority. During the following session, Mr. Ewing presented another majority report, accompanied by a bill
reorganizing the Post-Office Department, which passed the
Senate by a bare majority on the 9th of February, 1835.
This measure was defeated in the House of Representatives, and it was not until the following session, when
the Postmaster-General resigned, that the bill went into
operation.

Mr. Ewing was bitterly opposed to the removal of the
deposits from the United States Bank, regarding the
measure as unconstitutional.

It was through the instrumentality of Mr. Ewing that
the much-mooted question of the boundary of Ohio was
settled by a bill introduced by him December 21, 1835,
which reached its final passage the following year, on the
11th of March, in the Senate, and on the 15th of June in
the House of Representatives.

He also brought forward a bill for the reorganization
of the Land Office, which was passed during the same
session. He opposed the policy of granting pre-emption
rights, the admission of Michigan into the Union, and
discussed the complications which arose with the French
Government; spoke upon the deposit bill, the limitation
of executive patronage, and the fortification bill. He
also presented a memorial praying for the abolition of
slavery and the slave-trade in the District of Columbia,

and asked that it be appropriately referred, at the same
time expressing himself opposed to the granting of the
prayer of the memorialists.

In December, 1836, Mr. Ewing introduced a bill which
caused warm debate, and was ultimately defeated. This
was a measure for annulling a document issued by the
Secretary of the Treasury the previous year, called the
"Specie Circular," which authorized the receivers in the
Land Office to accept payments only in gold, silver, or
Treasury certificates, except from certain classes of persons, for a limited time. Another bill, declaring it un-
lawful for the Secretary to make discriminations, was
also defeated.

Mr. Ewing returned to Lancaster, and resumed the
practice of the law. Upon the election of General Harrison to the Presidency, Mr. Ewing, who had been a warm
supporter, was made a member of the Cabinet, occupy-
ing the position of Secretary of the Treasury, the duties
of which responsible office he continued to discharge under President Tyler.

His first official report was distinguished by the ad-
vocacy of measures intended to diminish the national
debt, one of which was the imposition of 20 per cent.
ad valorem duties on certain articles. In this report, he
also attacked the Independent Treasury Act, passed the
previous year, and advocated the establishment of a National Bank. Mr. Ewing subsequently drafted a bill for
the establishment of a National Bank, which was vetoed
by the President.

At the request of President Tyler, Mr. Ewing then drafted a charter, which passed both Houses of Congress, but was also vetoed. Thereupon the entire Cabinet, with the exception of Mr. Webster, resigned. Mr. Ewing published a letter explaining his views and giving the reason for the course he had taken.

The Department of the Interior having been created under the administration of President Taylor, Mr. Ewing accepted the Secretaryship, and organized it. During his term of office, he recommended several measures of public importance in his reports.

Mr. Ewing differed from Mr. Clay and others of his associates on the question of Congressional legislation on the subject of slavery. Mr. Clay contended that the question should be settled at once, and Mr. Ewing that the legislation of Congress was uncalled for.

The death of General Taylor and the accession of Mr. Fillmore, on the 9th of July, 1850, precipitated the question, and rendered the resignation of Mr. Ewing necessary. Hon. Thomas Corwin was appointed Mr. Ewing's successor, and Mr. Ewing was appointed by the Governor of Ohio to serve in the Senate the unexpired term of Mr. Corwin. During this period, he was an active defender of General Taylor's Administration. He was opposed to the fugitive slave law, the compromise bill of Mr. Clay, advocated the establishment of a branch mint in California, the reduction of postage, internal improvements, and various other measures of public importance.

He did not retire to private life until 1851, when he returned to Lancaster, his old home, and resumed the practice of the law. He was engaged as an attorney in many important litigations requiring the exercise of the highest order of talent, and always acquitted himself with distinguished credit. His ability as a lawyer was only excelled by his ability as a public speaker and a statesman.

About a week ago, he embraced the religion of the Catholic Church, and received the sacrament at the hands of Archbishop Purcell.

[Washington Patriot.]

DEATH OF HON. THOS. EWING, OF OHIO.

The following despatch has been received from General Sherman :

"LANCASTER, OHIO, Oct. 26.

"Hon. Thomas Ewing died at half-past three o'clock this afternoon, surrounded by his family, as easily and naturally as though taking a sleep. He will be buried here at 11 o'clock on Saturday.   W. T. SHERMAN."

Since the deaths of Douglas, Crittenden, and Taney, the country has been called to mourn the loss of no states-man of equal power and national fame. His eminent public services merit and demand a more detailed notice than the mere mention of the day and hour of his death.

He was born in Virginia, December 28, 1789, of

Revolutionary parentage. In his third year his father removed to that portion of the frontier settlements which is now the State of Ohio. His youth and early manhood were passed amid the hardships of frontier life. His studies were pursued by the light of a hickory bark, and by the earnings of his manual labor he paid for his father's farm and his own education.

In 1816, one year after graduating at the Ohio University, he was admitted to the bar. He was then twenty-seven years of age, and immediately rose to eminence, verifying the maxim that "the law has hopes of those who come to it late." He was a Whig Senator in 1831, and again in 1850, to fill the unexpired term of Thomas Corwin. During his political career he sustained nearly all the Whig party measures. He was actively engaged in 1834 in reorganizing the Post-Office; brought in the bill for the reorganization of the General Land Office; and introduced and passed the bill for the settlement of the Ohio Boundary question. In 1840, he became Secretary of the Treasury under General Harrison, continuing under Tyler, but resigned upon the veto of the National Bank Bill, a measure which he favored, having himself prepared a bill for the establishment of the bank. As Secretary of the Interior under Taylor, in 1849, he organized the then new Interior Department, and originated and recommended its earliest measures of internal progress and development. Since 1851 he has lived retired from public life.

His celebrity as a statesman and public speaker is

equalled by his reputation as a lawyer. His leading mental quality was that of great clearness and compactness of reasoning. Arguments whereon other equally eminent lawyers would consume days, he would condense within half an hour, for which he was often complimented from the bench. These powers of his mind have secured for him the title of the " Great Logician of the West." In person, he was tall and commanding and possessed of a powerful frame; in manner, quiet, self-controlled, gentle, and courteous; always exhibiting one of the most endearing marks of true greatness—kindness and consideration for youth.

In his late years he has taken no very active part in politics, though he has not unfrequently given to the country the wise advice of conciliation and harmony. He sustained the election of Mr. Lincoln, and the patriotic prosecution of the war, for pure and national purposes, but he was earnestly opposed to the Radical measures of reconstruction, and to their unconstitutional legislation since the war; and during and since the administration of President Johnson, he has avowedly thought and acted with the Democracy.

The friend and compeer of Clay and Webster, he may be pronounced almost the last of a great race of states-men, who, deeply learned in the history, laws, and Constitution of their country, and identified with its institutions since their creation, were inspired by a devoted love for their country, and could never tolerate any violation of the spirit or letter of the Constitution. He was always steadily opposed to executive encroachments, and made this opposition one of his fundamental political principles.

He leaves behind him a family, large, powerful, and established in the love, confidence, and respect of the entire country. While the country has thus lost one of its "pillars of state," they have lost a father, a counsellor, and a friend, who, renewing his youth in them, has heretofore added to the strength and vigor of their manhood the wisdom of his years and the counsels of his experience. The country deeply mourns his loss, and tenders its sympathies and condolence to his afflicted family. While he lived, he commanded the respect of age and the reverence and attachment of youth; and, dying in the fulness of years, his head is thrice silvered with honor, dignity, and fame.

[Cincinnati Commercial.]

DEATH OF THOMAS EWING.

This event took place at Lancaster last Thursday afternoon. Elsewhere a memoir, prepared by one of his old friends, is published. It is interesting, especially on account of the beautiful and instructive story told of the boyhood and early manhood of Mr. Ewing. All have heard of him as the "Salt-Boiler," but few of this generation have known with what honorable toil and with what admirable ambition that title was earned.

In public life, he stood high among the strong men.

13

His first term in the United States Senate was from March 4, 1831 ; and he was succeeded by William Allen, who was elected by one majority. He was very active on the stump for Harrison in 1840, for Clay in 1844, and for Taylor in 1848. He was in the Cabinets both of Harrison and Taylor. After the death of Harrison, he bitterly resented the partisan defection of Tyler; and after Taylor's death he preferred the Senate to the Cabinet. Then Corwin became Secretary of the Treasury, under Fillmore, and Ewing was appointed Senator to fill the vacancy occasioned by Corwin's resignation.

It is related that after the nomination of General Taylor by the Whig Convention, the triumphant Taylor men, anxious to conciliate Mr. Clay's friends, proposed the nomination of Mr. Ewing for Vice-President, and it would have followed as a matter of course, had not the Hon. L. D. Campbell, inconsolable for the defeat of Clay, and irritated too, declared that Ohio "did not want any sugar-plums," and the nomination passed on to Fillmore, and made him President.

Mr. Ewing's resolute adherence to the course that his own convictions marked out for him was strikingly apparent in his opposition to Henry Clay's great compromise measure, known as the Omnibus Bill. Mr. Clay exerted his whole strength to bring support to that bill, and on one occasion intimated strongly to Mr. Ewing that he would suffer for his opposition to it, succeeding only in drawing from him a positive expression of antagonism to his policy. In this memorable contest,

Mr. Ewing was against the Fugitive-slave Law and in favor of the unconditional admission of California as a State. When the time came that Mr. Ewing was a candidate for re-election to the Senate, owing to the personal opposition of General J. H. Geiger, he lacked a vote or two of having enough. The result was, after a fierce struggle, the election of a gentleman not then well known in the State, but who happened to have three or four fast friends. His name was Benjamin F. Wade.

In his retirement from official life, Mr. Ewing did not lose interest in public affairs. He was active in his profession, and his force of character and intellect gave him unsought conspicuity and influence. In 1861, he was appointed by Governor Denison to represent Ohio in the Peace Commission, which sat in Washington. His associates were S. P. Chase, Reuben Hitchcock, F. T. Backus, and Judge J. C. Wright. When hostilities broke out, he took an active part in favor of measures for the support of the National Government, and throughout the war was an earnest supporter of the Government and a trusted counsellor of President Lincoln, whose regard for him amounted to veneration. On the Trent seizure, with Slidell and Mason, he immediately wrote Mr. Lincoln, "There is no such thing as contraband of war between neutral ports," and urged that Mason and Slidell be surrendered to the English in accordance with international law. When Mr. Everett's opinion was published, arguing that our Government had a right to hold them under the law of nations, Mr. Ewing hurried to Washington, and found Mr. Seward inclined to Mr. Everett's view, but Mr. Lincoln felt from the first a doubt about the right of our Government to retain them. Mr. Ewing's great influence—those who know best how ardently it was exerted, have reason to believe—turned the scale, and we were saved from a rash and needless war with England, at a time that would have called for tremendous sacrifices, and that might have destroyed our national unity.

In 1862, Mr. Ewing formed a new partnership, and entered upon the practice of the law in Washington City; but at the close of the war he retired from the practice, except as to a few old cases. In arguing one of these, something more than a year ago, it will be remembered, he fell in a fainting-fit from over-exertion and the effects of the malady which has occasioned his death.

He retained his faculties to the last in a remarkable degree. He has, occasionally, during several years, in addressing the public, preferred to do it through the columns of this journal. At his advanced age, his massive communications, all written out with his own firm hand, were literary and MS. curiosities, and bore testimony to his capacity for labor and the unabated force of his faculties. Always of a conservative tendency, though his natural disposition was at once impetuous and imperious, he had a lawyer's dread and detestation of revolutionary proceedings; and he could not see the necessity, or believe in the safety, of the reconstructive legislation of Congress. This drove him to act during his last days with the Democratic party.

A few months ago, he gave the old homestead at Lancaster, which had been his home since 1823, to Thomas Ewing, Jr., and last summer, knowing full well his condition, and feeling that the end of his days drew nigh, he revisited the scenes of his boyhood, and with touching tenderness revived old associations, after an absence from them of more than half a century.

Public life prevented Mr. Ewing realizing the full pecuniary rewards from his professional labors that his reputation would have commanded; but he was, in his old age, in the enjoyment of a comfortable competency. As a statesman, austere and inflexible; as a partisan, passionate and resolute, and not always exercising the completest self-control, he was a considerate and kindly friend; and his devotion to the memory of his wife, and love for and pride in his children, beautified his life.

[Mansfield Herald.]

HON. THOMAS EWING.

The country, on Thursday, lost, in the death of Thomas Ewing, the last link that bound the present political era to the dim and fading past. Mr. Ewing died calmly at his residence in Lancaster, O., which has been his home for more than half a century,

and where all his children were born, and all were
with him at his death.   Biographies have already
been published in the Cincinnati papers, and read by
many of the readers of the *Herald*, but as the writer
of this knew him well, he thinks that a more extended
sketch than has been presented, embracing some incidents that have not been named in these, might
not be uninteresting.

Mr. Ewing was born near West Liberty, Virginia,
in 1789, his father having moved into that country
in 1786.   This place is situated about six miles east
of the Ohio River, and was then the most densely
populated place, south of Pittsburg, near the river.
It is no more thickly settled now than then.   The
house where he was born was removed long before
he was.   When he was but three years old, his father
removed to Ohio and bought land on the Muskingum
River, where he lived for some years, then removed
to Federal Creek, where he lived until his son had
made money enough by the law to buy and settle
him on a good farm in Indiana.   Thomas labored
hard upon the farm, but yearned for a higher life.
With all his labor and deprivation of intellectual resources, he found time to read and study, and the
more he studied, the more he desired.   He had a
few months' schooling at West Liberty in 1797, and
subsequently had six months' teaching at a small school
near his home, and this was all until he was twenty
years of age.   His whole time was spent in hard

labor on a farm until he was nineteen years old,
when he went to the Kanawha River, in Virginia, and
there went to boiling salt. This was about 200 miles
from his home, and in a country that is still wild
and sparsely populated, yet, besides having salt in
abundance, is one of the richest mineral regions in
the Union. Here he earned $80 in four months, which
he gave to his father, but spent part of the ensuing
winter at Athens, and in the next two years earned
nearly enough to enable him to graduate at Athens
College, then the only one in the State. After many
struggles and privations, he graduated in 1815, and
received the first degree of A.B. ever conferred in
the State. He was then twenty-six years of age, and
had still his profession to study without money. He
commenced to study with Gen. Beecher, of Lancaster,
and was admitted to the bar at twenty-eight years
of age. He at once took a high position as a sound
lawyer and powerful advocate. He seemed to grasp
all the strong points of his cases, and was able to
set them forth in such a manner as to convince the
reason, not influence the passions, of the court and
jury. He made use of none of the tricks of the
trade. All with him was straightforward, earnest
truth, which he preserved throughout his political
as well as legal and domestic life.

In person, Mr. Ewing was large and robust, but
never fleshy. His frame had been fully developed
with manual labor in his younger life, and his man-

ner and all his movements, as well as his language,
gave you that impression, as both did of the earnestness and truthfulness of his character. Although many
of the early members of the bar of Ohio became
eminent entirely through their own exertions, and without early advantages of education, as Hammond, Corwin, and others, yet there are none to whom we could
so conscientiously direct the attention of the young
and ambitious as to Mr. Ewing. His early life seems
to have been one of settled purpose and blameless,
truthful energy, acquiring therein habits and tones
of thought and strong filial affections that marked him
through life.   Young men, especially you to whom
the world before you looks cold and hard, and hopes
vague and dim, remember Thomas Ewing, " the salt-
boiler," and follow him in fixedness of purpose, strength
of will, perseverance, and, above all, in strict integrity
and temperance of life and habits, and the clouds,
though dense, will clear away and a bright sunlight
will beam upon your future lives and hearts.

In 1830, Mr. Ewing was elected to the Senate of
the United States with great unanimity by the Legislature of Ohio,` not because he was a politician, nor
because he had an influential family or connections,
but simply because they knew him capable. Without any special attractions of eloquence in voice,
language, or manner, Mr. Ewing at once took position among the highest in that bright galaxy of
statesmen in which were Clay, Webster, Calhoun,

Preston, Bayard, and Benton.   He was then but little more than forty years old—among the youngest
of the eminent men, but his ability was at once
acknowledged.   He looked older—indeed, seemed never
to have had a youth.   He spoke but rarely, nay,
only when it seemed necessary to carry an important point.   His speeches are still extant against
the confirmation of Van Buren to the Court of St.
James, the removal of the deposits, in favor of a
protective tariff, the re-charter of the United States
Bank, the Revenue Collection Bill, the Ohio Boundary
question, on the admission of Michigan, and on various other questions.   His language was always plain
as his manner, but always to the point.   His manner and style were between those of Webster, Davis,
Preston, and Crittenden, and partook of some and
lacked some of the qualities of each.   In a word, it
seemed like that of a man who says, "I am going
to cut that tree down before dinner," and goes syste-
matically about it.

Mr. Ewing was simply neat enough in his dress
to show that observing propriety was all he cared
about, and paid no further attention to it.   Such
was the fact with nearly all the prominent men of
that day.   Mr. Van Buren, who took his seat as Vice-
President in 1833, was the most fastidious in dress,
rather foppish for a man of his age, but he had
very good taste in adapting colors to his foxy com-
plexion.

11

At the expiration of his first term, the Democracy being in the ascendant, Wm. Allen was elected in his place. In 1841, Gen. Harrison called him to the head of the Treasury Department. Harrison dying at the end of a month, John Tyler became President. He was weak, and although he had said, both publicly and privately, before and after his inauguration, that he should, in case of a tie in the Senate, vote in favor of the charter of a United States Bank, he announced to his cabinet that he would only sign one with the privilege of branches in the States consenting thereto. Mr. Ewing drafted and submitted a bill with that feature, which Mr. Clay and his friends rejected, and re-passed the old bank charter. This was vetoed under the influence of the Democracy that crowded around Tyler, and Mr. Ewing, seeing the failure of Tyler's administration, resigned. This was done, we happen to know, not because he justified Congress in rejecting the bill which he knew was the only one that would be signed, but because he knew that Mr. Tyler could not be relied on, and the swarm of toadies that had Mr. Tyler's ear destroyed his influence with the President.

He remained in private life from 1841 to 1849, and few men so perfectly retained the respect and admiration of the people of the country as he did. In 1849, he was at once selected by Gen. Taylor as head of the Department of the Interior—a department then being organized, and the heaviest and most intricate

in our government.   On the death of Gen. Taylor
and the incoming of Mr. Fillmore, he again resigned,
and was appointed to the vacancy in the Senate occasioned by the resignation of Mr. Corwin, whose
term closed in 1851, when Mr. Ewing retired to the
practice of his profession, in which he remained until
his death.

Mr. Ewing's resignation of his position in Mr. Fillmore's cabinet and his opposition to the Omnibus Bill,
which failed, and to the Fugitive-slave Bill in particular, would seem to indicate an opposition to Mr.
Clay; but they were firm friends until Mr. Clay's
death.   Mr. Clay incorporated the Fugitive-slave Bill
in his omnibus or compromise bill—it being drawn by
Mr. Mason, of Virginia—because it was the only measure that could prevent the South from rebellion at
that time, and to preserve the Union.   Mr. Clay adopted
it, and pushed it through by his influence with the
North.   Mr. Clay and Mr. Ewing regarded the bill in
the same light, as unconstitutional and perversive of
all law and right, and Mr. Ewing refused to support
it, let the South do what they might.   Mr. Clay thought
a peaceful union required any sacrifice.

In the analysis of Mr. Ewing's qualities, we find
powerful physical development aided by early labor
and preserved by regular and correct habits and practices of life, an affectionate but not demonstrative
feeling, an intellect slow and cautious to work, but
powerful to grasp all points, and a sterling and un-

flinching integrity of purpose and action. He was
an instructive more than an agreeable and pleasing
conversationalist, for he lacked buoyancy and versa-
tility, which would have destroyed his usefulness but
for his unflinching perseverance. Few men are more
happy in their family relations than was Mr. Ewing,
and his memory will long be cherished by a large
circle of friends, and revered by historians.

DEATH OF HON. THOMAS EWING.

Among the notable events of this period that history will record, is the death of the distinguished
citizen whose name is at the head of this brief
notice.

Thomas Ewing died at his residence in Lancaster,
Ohio, on Thursday, the 26th inst., at the age of about
82 years.   On Saturday, the 28th, his remains were
committed to the tomb with the religious ceremony
of the Catholic Church, and an eloquent address and
eulogy pronounced by Archbishop Purcell.   The funeral
was attended by U. S. Senators Sherman and Thurman,
Governor Hays and several of the State officers, the
Judges of the Supreme Court, and many other distinguished gentlemen from adjacent counties, among
whom were many leading members of the bar.   Also,
by the City Council of the city of Lancaster, and the

judges and lawyers of the county in a body. Among the pall-bearers were Honorables H. H. Hunter, Henry Stanbery, Gov. R. B. Hayes, A. G. Thurman, John Sherman, Henry B. Curtis, Judge Welch, C. B. Goddard, John H. James, Charles Borland, John T. Brazee, and others—all selected from his life-time friends, and chiefly from the bar of Fairfield and other counties in which for so many years he had labored with them, in the same profession.

The scene was very impressive as the great crowd of citizens and friends filled the lawns and streets in front of the mansion, and pressed their way in long files through the hall and room where the remains of the illustrious deceased were reposing in state, to take a last look of one so much beloved for his private virtues — so honored for his distinguished services.

All the immediate members of the deceased's family were present at his death, and in the funeral attendance—among whom was specially noticeable his distinguished son-in-law, General W. T. Sherman.

Mr. Ewing's family was formerly from Cumberland County, New Jersey. The subject of this notice was born near the village of West Liberty, Ohio County, Va. (now West Virginia), on the 28th of December, 1789. His parents (having lost in the times of the Revolution the estate inherited) moved to Ohio in April, 1792, and at first settled on the Muskingum River, but subsequently made their permanent

location on a little tract of land, on Federal Creek, in
Athens County. This was the home of Mr. Ewing's
boyhood days. Here by the side of his father he
learned to work. Here he toiled, as none but those
who have experienced like disadvantages can appreciate, to lay the foundation of that learning and
knowledge that afterwards adorned the court-room and
the forum, and held listening multitudes in rapt attention.

Mr. Ewing was emphatically the architect of his
own fortune. Every step he made in procuring an
education was sustained by the earnings of his own
rustic and manual labor. And when at last he attained his collegiate degree of A.B., he carried into
the study of his future profession, and in his subsequent practice, the same laborious habits of application and assiduity of study that are ever sure to win
success. He was called to the bar in 1817. His
early practice brought him into forensic contact with
the Beechers, the Irwins, the Shermans, Grangers, Stan-
berys, Sillimans, Swans, and McDowells of that day
—all men of experience, high talent, and great legal
acumen. But the mathematical mind and trained
habits of industry of the young lawyer Ewing were
equal to the demand, and he soon rose to command
the respect and confidence of the court and bar, wherever he practised. His professional engagements soon
made a circuit for him embracing a range of counties
extending from the river to the lakes; but more es-

pecially for his constant and regular attendance at the
terms of court, besides his own county of Fairfield,
the counties of Muskingum, Knox, Licking, Hocking,
Athens, Franklin, Pickaway, Jackson, etc.   It was in
this broad field, and as a county court lawyer, that
Mr. Ewing established his great fame at the bar, and
placed himself acknowledgedly at the head of his profession in the State of Ohio.   His subsequent career
in the higher courts of the State, and in the Supreme Court of the United States, gave him the
same enviable distinction in a wider sphere of usefulness.

His elevation to high and distinguished political or
civil positions was but the natural fruit and result of
the well-earned fame acquired in his profession.   He
was no tyro when he entered political life.   He graced
the positions to which he was called rather than received honor from them.   He did not seek office—
but was called to it by the demand of the best men
of the times.   He filled one full term in the United
States Senate, from 1831 to 1837 ; and was at a later
period appointed to fill the unexpired term of Thomas
Corwin in the same body.   "There were giants in
those days."   Mr. Ewing soon stood, not only the com·
peer in rank, but in talent, influence, and acknowledged
greatness, the equal of such men as Clay, Calhoun,
Webster, Benton, Hayne, Wright, and many others of
that period, whose master-minds and great acts have
left their impress upon the character of our institu-

tions and the history of our country.   Nor was our
deceased friend less distinguished as a public minister
in the several Cabinets of Presidents Harrison, Tyler,
Taylor, and Fillmore.   His comprehensive mind and
broad and liberal views looked far into the future, and
his recommendations were always marked by wisdom.

We cannot extend this article—our limits forbid.
We will close with the remark that Mr. Ewing's private life was without reproach.   Genial in disposition,
cheerful in manners, he made himself loved for his
goodness of heart, as well as respected and honored
for his noble qualities of mind.   To him may justly
be applied the sentiment best expressed in his own
law Latin:

> "*Suaviter in modo, fortiter in re.*"
>
>   B.

THE LATE THOMAS EWING.

Among the great men of Ohio who have stood in
the front rank at the bar, on the hustings, and in the
national councils, Thomas Ewing was one of the most
eminent.   As a lawyer, he has had few if any superiors
in the United States, and as a statesman, he has received
high recognition and honor.   Having a physical constitution of rare vigor, he retained his faculties in a
remarkable degree beyond the age of fourscore.   Though
a victim of heart disease for many years, it was but

recently that there were any decisive signs that nature was giving way. His mind was clear and strong to the last. For a week past, it has been known that his end must be near. At his old residence at Lancaster, with all his children about him, Mr. Ewing passed away about four o'clock last evening.

Thomas Ewing was born near the town of West Liberty, Ohio County, now West Virginia, on the 28th of December, 1789. His father had been a soldier in the Revolution, and when he left the army was possessed of little property. He remained in Virginia but a few years after his marriage, having removed in 1792 to the Muskingum Valley, when the subject of this sketch was less than three years old, and, not long after, to lands seventeen miles northwest of the frontier settlements, in what is now Athens County. Here Thomas passed his youth, on a farm in the wilds. Having been instructed in reading by an elder sister, he eagerly perused all the books within his reach, and acquired an inclination for the career afterwards pursued. When in his twentieth year he left home—the better to accomplish his wishes—and was employed in the Kanawha salt-works, where he saved money enough, in two or three years, to complete the payment for his father's land, leaving a surplus with which to start on a collegiate course at the Ohio University, at Athens. He was the first to receive the Bachelor's degree at that institution, in 1815.

He studied law, and was admitted to the bar at

Lancaster in 1816, where he continued to reside, practising in all the higher courts, with the eminent success
so well known. In 1830, he was elected to the United
States Senate, taking his seat the following year. A
Whig in politics, he co-operated actively with Clay
and Webster in opposition to the policy of Jackson.
One of his first speeches was made in opposition to
the confirmation of Martin Van Buren as Minister to
England. He supported the protective tariff policy
of Clay, advocated a reduction of the rates of postage,
a recharter of the National Bank, and the passage
of the Force Bill as a remedy for nullification. Among
the prominent measures with which he was identified
during this term of senatorial service was his bill for
reorganizing the Post-Office Department, which passed
the Senate without a division on the 9th of February,
1835, though it was lost in the House. The Postmaster-General, Barry, soon after resigned, and the
Department was reorganized under Amos Kendall, its
head being raised to the rank of a Cabinet Minister.
He introduced a bill for the settlement of the Ohio
Boundary question, which passed in 1836, and was
author of the act for reorganizing the General Land
Office, which became a law the same year. He pre
sented a petition for the abolition of slavery, insisting
that it ought to be received, though he was opposed
to the views of the memorialists. He also took a
leading part in the discussion of the once famous
" specie circular," issued by Levi Woodbury, Secretary

of the Treasury, in July, 1836, and which was long
an exciting topic throughout the country.

Mr. Ewing resumed the practice of his profession
in 1837, on the expiration of his senatorial term. He
was selected by President Harrison, in 1840, as Secretary of the Treasury, and continued in that office
under Mr. Tyler until September of that year, when
all the Cabinet officers, except Webster, resigned.
President Taylor, on coming into office in 1849, appointed Mr. Ewing as Secretary of the new Department of the Interior, which was as yet unorganized.
Again the death of a President terminated his cabinet
service, having resigned on Mr. Fillmore's assuming
the Executive chair, on the 9th of July, 1850.

After filling out the unexpired term of Mr. Corwin,
who resigned his seat in the Senate to become Secretary
of the Treasury, Mr. Ewing retired to Lancaster in
1851, since which time, almost to the day of his death,
he had been actively engaged in the practice of his
profession.

In public and private life, Mr. Ewing was a man
of integrity, determined in his purposes, powerful as
a friend or as an antagonist, dignified yet genial in
his bearing, strong but not hasty in his impulses,
and firmly attached to what he deemed the "good
old ways," in preference to change in the name of progress. A few days since, he was received into the
communion of the Roman Catholic Church, to which
his family belong. He retained his mental powers with

great clearness to the last, and quietly sank to rest from his prolonged earthly career.

[Toledo Commercial.]

HON. THOMAS EWING.

The despatches of Thursday night announced the death of this eminent Ohio jurist and statesman. He died at half-past three o'clock on the 26th inst., at his residence in Lancaster, of heart disease, or an accumulation of fatty matter about the heart—a disease which has prostrated him on several occasions during the past ten years. He was nearly eighty-two years of age, and died with all his children and many other members of his family around him, and with his mind clear and vigorous to the last. For more than a generation past he has filled a large space in the public eye, and has been recognized as one of the ablest jurists of his time, and as a statesman is to be ranked in the category with Clay and Webster, with whom he long served in the councils of the nation.

Mr. Ewing was born in Ohio County, Virginia, on the 28th day of December, 1789. His father had taken part in the struggle for American Independence, and in 1792, owing to his reduced circumstances, he removed to Ohio and settled in Athens County. An elder sister taught the boy Thomas to read, who, until his twentieth year, labored on his father's farm and read books at night by the light of a hickory fire. He then

left home and worked two or three years in the
Kanawha salt-works, and until he had accumulated a
sufficient sum to pay for his father's farm and to enable
him to enter the Ohio University, where he took the
degree of A.B., being the first graduate of the institution. He was emphatically the architect of his own
fame and fortune; and, in addition to acquiring a
collegiate education and a profession, he had the purpose
and strength, amid his early struggles and privations, to
purchase a farm for his father, and place the family
in comfortable circumstances. He "honored his father
and his mother," and he has, in turn, been honored
by his children, and his days have been "long in
the land," in strict fulfilment of the promise—a lesson,
by the by, which should not be lost upon young
men struggling against adverse circumstances. Nor
need such envy the more fortunate who have their
way paid through college, and frequently through
life. It is out of such early struggles and privations
that giants like Ewing come. Mr. Ewing studied
law with Philemon Beecher, a distinguished lawyer
of his day, at Lancaster, and was admitted to the bar
in 1816. His attention is said to have been turned
to the law during his boyhood. On one occasion (so
the story runs) he was driving his father's ox-team
by the court-house, in which an important case was
being tried. He stopped the team and entered the
court-room, where he remained to hear the argument
which the counsel made in behalf of the prisoner.

He was struck with the imperfectness of the defence, and, remarking that he could make a better plea himself, went out with the determination to become a lawyer.

During his early years at the bar, Mr. Ewing was distinguished as a hard student, and his close application to his books became a jest among the good-natured lawyers of those days, who rode from county to county on horseback, and trusted more to "inspiration" than to study for their success at the bar. He was not one of those who trusted to his "genius" to see him through, and hence he was always prepared, and nearly always successful. He was distinguished as much for the thoroughness of his legal knowledge as for his legal grasp and acumen; and it is said that, on one occasion, when he had an important case to prepare, he shut himself up in his room and remained there an entire week, and until he had mastered the case. Another "moral" which is pointed by his career is that great and permanent success is achieved only by hard labor. This is, perhaps, still more strikingly illustrated in the career of his early associate in the law, the now distinguished Hocking H. Hunter, who failed at first in several attempts to practise law, and returned to manual labor; but, having faith in himself and in hard study, he again took up the law, and has pushed his way to that "top story" in which Mr. Webster remarked that there was "always room."

Mr. Ewing was undoubtedly a great man, so far as greatness consists in massive power; but his chief

eminence was in the law, and his special power or
forte lay in real-estate cases. By his success in some
of these, he acquired the title to lands of great value.
Not the least among his important real-estate cases,
and in which he prepared elaborate arguments, was
that of Oliver *v.* Piatt *et al.*, involving the title to
a large part of Toledo.

Mr. Ewing's legal opinion was constantly sought and
liberally paid for from all parts of the country. He was
one of the most trusted advisers of President Lincoln in
matters of public policy, as well as upon points of law,
and his despatch to the President stating the law in the
Mason-Slidell case will be remembered. Within the
limits of an ordinary business despatch, he gave the
whole law of the case in the following words: "There
can be no contraband of war in a neutral bottom going
from one neutral port to another."

As a statesman, Mr. Ewing has always been ranked
as a conservative. He has never been recognized as one
of the "earnest" or "progressive" men of his time; yet
his record shows that during his second term in the
United States Senate (from 1850 to 1851) he refused to
vote for the Fugitive-slave Law, helped to defeat Mr.
Clay's Compromise Bill, and advocated the abolition of
slavery in the District of Columbia. During his first
Senatorial term (from 1831 to 1837), he was associated
with Clay and Webster in resisting Executive encroachments, and he supported the protective tariff system of
Mr. Clay.

In massive strength, physical and intellectual, he was the peer of Webster; and the two giants agreed mainly in their views of public policy. But Mr. Ewing lacked the oratorical grace and power of Webster, and compensated for this by greater independence and a more rugged self-respect. He lacked also the qualities of a popular leader, and his career as a statesman has been one of influence rather than of power. In other words, he has not held the public positions which give men power, but has exerted a vast influence over those who did hold such positions. He voted twice for Mr. Lincoln, and during the war was one of the chief Aarons who upheld the hands of the Presidential Moses, until the sun set upon a conquered Rebellion.

In March, 1831, Mr. Ewing took his seat in the United States Senate, where he remained until 1837. During this term he opposed the confirmation of Mr. Van Buren as Minister to England; supported the protective tariff system of Mr. Clay; advocated a reduction of postage, and secured a reorganization of the Post-Office Department; advocated the re-charter of the U. S. Bank, and opposed the removal of the deposits, by President Jackson; procured the passage of a bill settling the much-vexed Ohio Boundary question (out of which grew the famous "Toledo War"); and another reorganizing the General Land Office. He also opposed the admission of Michigan into the Union, and the granting of pre-emption rights to settlers on the public lands.

Mr. Ewing took an active part in the campaign of

1840, and achieved a national reputation as a stump
orator under the name of the "Old Salt-Boiler." Gen.
Harrison rewarded him by a seat in the Cabinet, where
he remained as Secretary of the Treasury under Tyler
until the latter forfeited the confidence of the Whigs,
when, with all the other members, except Mr. Webster,
Mr. Ewing resigned.   On the accession of General
Taylor to the Presidency, Mr. Ewing was again called
to the Cabinet; this time as Secretary of the Interior,
which department he organized.   When Mr. Fillmore
succeeded General Taylor, a change was made in the
Cabinet, Mr. Ewing retiring, but taking in the Senate
the place of Mr. Corwin, who was called to the Cabinet,
as Secretary of the Treasury.   Mr. Ewing filled the unexpired term of Mr. Corwin, and with the close of this
term (in 1851) his official career virtually ended.   He
was a Member of the Peace Congress in 1861, and, as
before stated, a warm supporter of Mr. Lincoln's administration; but, with his whole family, he favored the
reconstruction policy of President Johnson, and found
himself, after so many years of sturdy and uncompromis-
ing opposition, in action, if not in sympathy, with the
Democratic party.

For ten years Mr. Ewing was recognized as the leading man of the Whig party in Ohio, being their only
representative in the United States Senate between 1831
and 1845.   It was quite natural under the circumstances
that when, in the winter of 1844-5, his party again had
the choice of a Senator, he should expect to be returned
16

and so he would have been, but for the fact that in the meantime a competitor for partisan favor stronger in the elements of personal popularity appeared to dispute his claim. This was the distinguished "Tom Corwin," who, from his nomination for Governor in February, 1840, became the idol of his party. His more popular oratory and greater personal magnetism were not long in putting "Tom, the Wagoner Boy," in the place of the "Old Salt-Boiler." In 1848, Mr. Ewing was within a single vote of being the Whig nominee for Vice-President, in place of Mr. Fillmore, as he also was in 1850 of being the Senator instead of Ben. Wade. With this latter defeat, and the close of the fraction of a term he was then serving in the Senate, his political aspirations probably ceased.

As a man, Mr. Ewing was as pure as he was great. He had none of the vices nor distinguishing "weaknesses" of great men, and in his domestic relations was most fortunate and happy. He was married, in 1820, to Maria, daughter of Hugh Boyle, of Lancaster, who was a devout adherent of the Catholic Church, and distinguished in the church for her piety and charity. It is said of Mr. Ewing that in the early part of his legal career, when he was frequently away attending court, he would ride forty or fifty miles on Saturday and Saturday night, in order to be at home on Sunday to attend church with his family.

The children of Mr. Ewing, we believe, are all living,

and are an exception to the general rule, inasmuch as
they have inherited the brains as well as the name of
their father.   General Thomas Ewing, Jr., was distinguished during the war as the hero of Pilot Knob,
and his name has recently been before the people of
this State as the choice of the Democracy for Governor, though he was defrauded of the nomination by
the friends of Mr. McCook.   General Hugh Ewing
served through the war, and was Minister to the
Hague under Johnson.   General Charles Ewing took
an active part in the war, and is one of the noblest
Ewings of them all.   Judge Philemon Beecher Ewing
has been Judge of the Court of Common Pleas, during which service he was distinguished for the clearness and correctness of his decisions.   Mrs. General
Sherman and Mrs. Colonel Steele are both distinguished in private life for superior culture and character.   Mr. Ewing has been frequently charged by
his neighbors with having possessed inordinate family
pride.   Probably the fact that there was such good
ground for this pride, gave rise to the charge.   He
was most happy in his domestic relations, and probably no father was ever more beloved and respected by
his children.   He had a tender regard for their happiness.   He was profoundly versed in all the nobler
literature, his chief delight being in Shakespeare and
Milton, in whose works he was in the habit of drilling
his children.

The public will be glad to learn that some years

since, at the urgent request of his children, Mr. Ewing commenced an autobiography, which is understood to have been brought down to a recent time; but how complete it may be, we are not able to state. Such a work would constitute a valuable contribution to the history of the State and the country.

Mr. Ewing was nearly the last of those eminent lawyers who once made the Lancaster bar famous, as he was also nearly the last of those political giants of a former era who have had much to do in shaping the public opinion and the legislation of the present time. Ohio has had more successful politicians, but no greater statesman and jurist than Thomas Ewing.

A. P. M.

EWING'S FUNERAL.

On Saturday, October 28, 1871, the remains of the Hon. Thomas Ewing were consigned to their last resting-place.

The occasion calls for tribute to the memory of a great and virtuous man, and those surrounding him. It was the last shadow closing the eternal sunset of a brilliant life—one that had begun with all the hardships and trials of a friendless pioneer—one that without wealth or friends had gathered in the wild woods, or by the lonely cabin fire, a lore and a mental strength that made him the peer of Clay, Webster, Calhoun, or any other leader of a later day. It was the funeral of a great statesman—one that had left upon his country's history a name and character that shall remain "ages after each of us have passed away for ever"; and in offering the last solemn honors to his remains, there "were collected together the captains of armies, the leaders of parties, the oracles of senates, and the ornaments of courts."

And there present, too, were unknown men belonging to the early history of the State—men who had heard the wild wolf howl and the Indian yell while redeeming Ohio from the forest and the savage; and the living leaders of the present were joined at the funeral to the historic past by many a decrepit form in the "sere and yellow" belonging to a generation fast passing away.

There, too, were the grand old apostles of Catholicity in the West—Archbishop Purcell and Rev. Dominic Young—cheering the mournful farewell to the illustrious dead with the sweet consolations of religion, and uniting the historic memories of Ohio with the teachings published to wandering Judea by the lightnings of Sinai, and leading to honors not evanescent and to monuments not made by human hands. For more than fifty years the three had been friends, and they were at his bedside in his dying moments to "guide his wandering spirit home."

When Ewing was entering upon his remarkable career, and at a time when little of convenience and

nothing of luxury was known in our State, the venerable Archbishop was devoting his life to the service
of Heaven.   As Bishop, he had often travelled on horseback through our county and Southern Ohio, often
uncertain in the morning whether he would have more
than the bare ground for his couch at night, content
with corn-bread and venison for his evening repast.
and the cabin floor for his bed.   Like those from whom
his mitre descended to him, he was truly an apostle,
and asked nothing from this world, and truly lived
the "meek and lowly" life that was taught by Him
who died to save mankind.

And old Father Dominic—the one before whom
the dead statesman had plighted eternal love to his
sainted wife, long, long years before—was at his dying
bedside to plight his departing spirit to its eternal
Source.   He, too, is one of the historic characters that
are so fast leaving us — one that our citizens here
may well cherish as a "father in Israel"—the one
that first carried his creed from Catholic Maryland
to the then wilderness of Ohio.   Him we claim as
our own, in character and career.   More than fifty years
ago he planted the cross where St. Joseph's now is
—the first pioneer of the Catholic faith that followed
the French missionaries of the last century.   At that
time there was not a Catholic church in the State.
He saw the Indians and the wild wolf and deer
for ever abandon the country;   he saw and shared
with the early settler, half hunter and half farmer,

in his hard struggle with the wilderness; like the venerable Archbishop, he travelled many a day through pathless forests, on a mission of love, that extended almost from Vincennes to the Muskingum. His was not merely a life of teaching; it was also a manual struggle, axe in hand, to conquer a home for his people. Many a time did he put his shoulder to the log at raising the settler's cabin, and at rolling the logs in the "clearing."

Piety at this day never comes in connection with such matters: it etherealizes exclusively by theories.

He built a cabin church at St. Joseph's, and placed upon it the first bell that rung west of the Alleghanies, and it is preserved there still.

And these three brave old men were together for the last time; one dead, the others to bestow the last and holiest attentions that friendship can offer.

And all had been successful—all had lived to realize their dreams of youth when each was beginning. Ewing had bid the torch-light and cabin fire bring him power and fame, and they came at his command.

· Purcell and Young had asked of Him who rules all things to build up His altar in the wilderness, and it was built. "The wilderness blossomed as the rose"; their altars and followers became almost numberless. Bigotry and superstition were consigned to times long gone, and their illustrious friend, now dead, had come to believe as they believed, and to die as they would wish to die.

In those funeral rites was a panorama of all there can be of poetry, religion, and history.

These friends of a long life, these companions of many a suffering hour—the priest that had blessed the marriage-vow, when young, of the statesman of fourscore, and had cheered his fainting spirit over death's dark waters; the pioneers of Western civilization and the rulers of to-day, with the fame of the mighty dead around them; the triumphant present and the momentous past—all linked together, and listening to the *De Profundis* as it had been chanted over the dead long before the Western world was known.

So passes away all there is of life—so, like a drop in the ocean, or a snow-flake in the avalanche, never to be known again, each generation is lost to the rest.

Proceedings of the City Council

OF LANCASTER, OHIO.

[Ohio Eagle.]

IN MEMORIAM.

HON. THOMAS EWING departed this life a few days
since, in Lancaster, O. He graduated in 1815, receiving
the first degree given by the Ohio University, that of
A.B., when few students and fewer universities claimed
a place in the new West.

Of his college career we know but little; yet we know,
of a truth, that his difficulties were many, his conflicts
were fierce, and if his life was a success, he merits credit.

But Thomas Ewing's work is ended. His fittest
monument is the institutions of our country, which he
strove to perpetuate, and the inscription thereon:

LIBERTAS ET NATALE SOLUM.

' At a recent session of the Athenian Literary Society
of the Ohio University, the following resolutions were
adopted:

WHEREAS, This Society has heard with deep sorrow
the announcement of the death of Hon. Thomas Ewing,
one of its most venerable members; therefore,

17

Resolved, That in his death we lose an honored member, and the nation sustains an irreparable loss.

Resolved, That as a testimony of respect for his memory, we drape our hall in mourning for thirty days.

Resolved, That these resolutions be published in the Athens and Lancaster papers, and a copy be sent to the family of the deceased.

A. B. RICHARDSON,
E. M. JACKSON,
D. C. CASTO,

Oct. 30, 1871.   *Committee.*

CITY CLERK'S OFFICE, LANCASTER, O.,
October 30, 1871.

To the Family of the Hon. Thomas Ewing :

In pursuance of the resolution of the Council of this city, I herewith furnish you with a copy of their proceedings of the 27th inst. relative to the death of your lamented and beloved father.

COUNCIL CHAMBER OF THE CITY OF LANCASTER,
October 27, A.D. 1871.

Council met pursuant to a call of the President.

Members present—John L. Tuthill, Hugh Cannon, P. M. Wagenhals, George Hood, H. W. Develling, Jacob Walter, James Weaver, James Henley.

On motion, the reading of the minutes was dispensed with.

. Dr. P. M. Wagenhals moved that a committee of three be appointed to draft resolutions expressive of the sense of this Council as to the death of the Hon. Thomas Ewing.

Thereupon the President appointed the following committee:

P. M. Wagenhals, Jacob Walter, and Hugh Cannon.

The Committee reported the following, viz.:

"Ohio's greatest and noblest is no more! Thomas Ewing died yesterday. More than fourscore were his, yet his eye was not dimmed nor his mental vigor abated, until 'the silver cord of life was loosed' and 'the golden bowl was broken.'

"In early manhood he came among us, and with the interests of our city he has been identified for more than fifty years. He was our nation's wisest counsellor, and in her peril was her ardent and determined friend. He lived to see the enemies of our country vanquished, and rejoiced in their discomfiture and dismay. Ever loyal, ever true, ever just to his country, he fell after the sanguinary strife was over, after the wounds inflicted had been healed, and with his closing eyes beheld our country's standard high advanced and reverenced everywhere.

"*Resolved*, That the City Council of the City of Lancaster will attend the funeral of Hon. Thomas Ewing, deceased, on Saturday, 28th inst.

"*Resolved*, That the Council of the city recommend the suspension of all business from 11 A.M. until 1 P.M. on Saturday, 28th instant, and that the City Clerk be instructed to issue circulars to that effect immediately.

"*Resolved*, That the City Clerk be instructed to furnish a copy of the above proceedings to the family of the deceased.

"*Resolved*, That the editors of the State be requested to publish in their respective papers the above proceedings.

> "P. M. WAGENHALS,
> JACOB WALTER,
> HUGH CANNON,
> *Committee*."

On motion, That when the Council adjourn, it adjourn to meet at the Council Chamber at half-past ten o'clock A.M., and that they attend the funeral of the Hon. Thomas Ewing in a body.

On motion, Council adjourned.

JOHN L. TUTHILL,   Attest: W. L. KING,
    President.   *City Clerk.*

PROCEEDINGS OF THE BAR.

PROCEEDINGS OF THE BAR

Of Lancaster, Ohio, on the Occasion of the Death of Hon. Thomas Ewing.

Immediately on the organization of Court, the death, on the 26th of this month, of the Hon. Thomas Ewing, late a member of this Bar, was announced by Hon. H. H. Hunter, who presented the proceedings of the Lancaster Bar in that regard, and moved that the same be spread on the journal of the Court.

It was thereupon ordered by the Court, that said proceedings, and also the addresses of Mr. Hunter and others on the occasion, be placed on the journal in full.

The proceedings and addresses are as follows, to wit :

At a meeting of the Bar of Lancaster, at the office of the Clerk of our Common Pleas Court, on Friday evening, October 27, 1871, to consider suitable formal action to be taken by its members in relation to the decease and obsequies of their late distinguished and honored professional exemplar, the Honorable Thomas Ewing, all the members of the Bar were present.

An organization was formed by calling Hon. H.

H. Hunter to the chair, and appointing Tall Slough secretary.

Hon. C. D. Martin moved the appointment of a committee, to be named by the meeting, to draft appropriate resolutions in memory of the deceased, which motion was adopted. The following gentlemen were selected to constitute that committee, viz.: Hon. H. H. Hunter, Hon. John T. Brasee, Hon. P. Van Trump, Hon. M. A. Daugherty, John D. Martin, Esq., Wm. P. Creed, Esq., and Hon. C. D. Martin.

On motion of John S. Brasee, Esq., it was resolved that, when this meeting adjourn, it adjourn to meet at the Court House on next Monday morning at ten o'clock.

On motion of W. P. Creed, Esq., the committee on resolutions was instructed to report to the adjourned meeting, and that the proceedings of the Bar be presented to the Court by the Hon. H. H. Hunter, and that, in connection therewith, Mr. Hunter, the intimate friend and professional associate of the deceased, pronounce an eulogium upon his life and character.

K. Fritter, Esq., moved that the Lancaster Bar, in a body, attend the funeral of the deceased; which motion prevailed.

On motion of John S. Brasee, the meeting adjourned.

Monday morning, ten o'clock, Bar meeting convened, pursuant to adjournment.

The committee on resolutions submitted the following report, which was adopted, viz.:

"*Resolved*, That in the death of Thomas Ewing, the members of the Lancaster Bar, which he so long adorned, have lost not only an exemplar of every forensic excellence and of every professional virtue, but also a friend who, by his uniform kindness to his brethren, had won the affection of every heart.

"*Resolved*, That while his pre-eminent ability as a jurist was recognized throughout the State and the nation, his co-laborers in the field of his early efforts and of many of his triumphs, who knew well his powers and his methods, and were familiar with his every-day professional life, bear willing testimony to the solid and varied learning, the vast mental resources, the honest and untiring zeal, and the chivalric bearing at the bar, which fully entitled him to the almost unequalled fame which crowned his professional career.

"*Resolved*, That these qualities which graced him as a lawyer, combined with a natural aptitude for public affairs, and an ardent and unselfish patriotism, were found, upon his being called into the service of the nation, whether as Senator or Cabinet officer, to qualify him for the highest duties and place him in the front rank of statesmen.

"*Resolved*, That notwithstanding his distinction in these walks, it is yet his character as a private citizen, his purity of heart, his nobility of conduct, his firm adherence to the right without regard to consequences, his conscientious fulfilment of duty in every relation of life, his warm attachment and his abounding charity, to which his friends will ever point with fondest pride, and which, more than even his distinguished position as a public man, will, for all time, to those who knew him best, embalm his memory in an odor of sweetness."

On motion of John D. Martin, it was resolved that a transcript of these proceedings, including a copy of Hon. H. H. Hunter's eulogy of the deceased, be furnished by the secretary for publication in pamphlet form, and that copies thereof be transmitted by him to the family of the deceased.

On motion, the meeting adjourned.

H. H. HUNTER, *President.*

TALL SLOUGH, *Secretary.*

REMARKS OF HON. H. H. HUNTER.

May it please the Court :

I am instructed by the members of the Bar of this city to present to the Court resolutions adopted at a recent meeting held by them on the occasion of the death of our fellow-citizen, Hon. Thomas Ewing. I beg leave to read them, and move the Court to order them to be entered on the journal.

The proceedings of the bar I now present to the Court, and ask to have them read.

In presenting these resolutions, I take leave to submit a few remarks prompted by the occasion.

Our venerable brother—I should rather say the patriarch of our profession—whose death we commemorate, has long been amongst us, and has passed away full of years and full of honors, without spot or blemish —not cut off in the midst of life and active usefulness, but, like full-ripened fruit of goodly fragrance, has been gathered—his spirit to the Creator who gave it, his body to the grave.

The work he was sent to perform is finished, though much that he has done will live after him in the hearts and minds of those who knew him; and we are left, not to lament his death, for it is appointed of God for all once to die, but to rejoice that he lived.

Full-orbed, he shed his light in the world amongst men, and a world of men recognize it. Eminently wise as a statesman and philosopher, during long years after he ceased to occupy office and place in the public councils, he continued in his retirement to exert a powerful influence on the events and affairs of the nation, through the press and by confidential counsellings, sought by those in power, who knew and appreciated his wisdom and integrity of purpose.

The present does not seem to be an appropriate occasion to enter largely into details of his eventful public acts or private life, or to do more than to glance at them in a general way; and this the more especially because, as I am advised, arrangements are being made for a

meeting of the bar of the State in commemoration of
our deceased friend. And yet, as his fellow-townsmen
and professional brethren, it is meet and proper that
we honor his memory by placing on the records of
this Court these resolutions, and to communicate them
to his family.

On the occasion anticipated and referred to at the
opening of the next regular term of the Supreme Court
of the State at Columbus, when a full attendance of the
members of the bar of the State may be expected, the
details of the public official services of the honored
deceased, and his professional life and career, his general
characteristics as a man in the society of men, and as
neighbor and friend, and in his individual and private
relations, will, doubtless, be appropriately brought under
consideration.

Nevertheless, may it please the Court, it is fitting that
we, his professional brethren and neighbors, shall give
utterance to our thoughts on these topics whilst the
event of the closing of his life is fresh and recent upon
our minds.

More than half a century ago, our honored friend,
then in his early manhood, and when the humble
individual who now addresses you was yet a boy, came
to our then small village, a graduate of the Ohio University at Athens, having, by the results of his own
labor, secured to himself the means that enabled him
to obtain a collegiate education, and commenced the
study of law with General Philemon Beecher, an able

and successful practitioner.   He was admitted to the
bar in August, A.D. 1816, and became the copartner
of Mr. Beecher in the practice, and by the extraordinary
vigor of his intellect and unremitting application almost
immediately became the leader of the bar in Ohio,
competing successfully with the ablest and most experienced practitioners, and extending his practice widely
into different parts of the State and into the Federal
courts.

His chief employment in life, after being admitted
to the bar, was as a lawyer, till the year 1830, when
he was elected to the Senate of the United States; and
during his term of office, from 1831 to 1837, he devoted
his energies to the discharge of its duties—successfully,
by the force of his extraordinary intellectual vigor,
rising to a level of acknowledged equality as a statesman with Webster, Clay, Calhoun, and others, the
splendor of whose talents, and the extraordinary importance of the affairs of government which then occupied its attention, gave prominence to the Senate of
the United States, equal if not superior to any like
political body in the world.

The national history of the period, covering one of
the most important eras of its progress, involving the
discussion, agitation, and incipient settlement of the
great principles upon which the duration—nay, the
continued existence of the Union of the States under
the Constitution depended—could not be truthfully
written, did it not include, in the Senatorial galaxy

to which allusion has been made, the name of our departed friend, Thomas Ewing, as one of its brilliant stars.

And from that period, down almost to the closing scene of his life, his active, vigorous intellect, both in official station and in the retirement of private life, covering the period of the rise, progress, and suppression of the great rebellion of the so-called Confederate States, was employed in the cause of the country.

To no inconsiderable extent, it may be said that by his counsels battles have been fought, campaigns projected, and many of the leading measures of Government policy in the progress of the war suggested.

Firm and decisive in supporting the Union, and in suppressing the rebellion by the most energetic and efficient action, he was yet highly conservative in regard to the principles on which the revolted States should be reinstated, differing in this regard from the extreme radical policy of many of the supporters of the cause of the Union, with whom he had acted in the great contest. It thus happened that in those measures of policy to which he could not yield his assent in reconstructing the revolted States, he came to be regarded by the dominant party, with whom he had acted in suppressing the rebellion, as favoring its adherents rather than the legitimate Government.

In respect to this, much injustice has unwittingly been done to our departed friend.

Whatever may be the results of the dominant policy —an experiment not yet fully tested—it is the height of injustice to attribute to him any faltering in his devoted adherence to the legitimate government of the Union under the Constitution, moulded and shaped as it has been, or shall be, to adapt it to the exigencies of times and events, by the American people.

As said, these great national affairs continued to be subjects of weighty consideration with our departed friend, from the period of his entering the Senate in 1831 to the close of his life. But during that interval he also to a large extent, to within a recent period, kept up the practice of his profession, chiefly, however, in select cases of importance, and in the higher courts—his example in which is before us to stimulate our efforts to render our profession worthy of its great objects—the administration of justice between individuals, and the propagation amongst men of the obligations of civilized society regulated by law and order.

We have yet to notice the example of our departed friend in his more private relations, as neighbor and citizen—in short, as a man in the ordinary walks of life.

Unostentatious, yet dignified and affable, he mingled but little, outside of his own individual and family affairs, with the current incidents. In political party movements he scarcely participated at all—he med dled not with the "*wire-working*" machinery or the

" *ropes* "*;* and was, consequently, several times defeated —or, rather, the efforts of his friends were defeated in his nomination for office, when his success would probably have saved the country from much of the trouble it has encountered in several important respects.

When a public improvement or any object of public interest, or the advancement of public charities, called for patronage and support, he was prompt and liberal in contributing aid, and in devising the best means for their promotion. So, also, in private charities—he gave liberally when it was a merit or a duty, and in the most quiet way. Among his circle of friends, some of whom were struggling with adversity, he was bountiful in noticing and extending to them the means of relief.

Such, may it please the Court, are some of the outline features, briefly and feebly portrayed, of the characteristics of our honored departed friend.

It does not become me to scarcely allude to one other subject forming a part of the characteristics of this truly great man—his religious faith and predilections. Until recently before his death, he had not made any public profession, or formally united himself with any church; yet a consistent Christian in his walk in life, and learnedly conversant with the doctrines of the Bible, and the whole body of church literature—for his was a mind that did not investigate by halves, or understand imperfectly—he closed the scene of his earthly existence by formally uniting himself with the church of his choice.

May he rest in peace!

May it please your Honor:

There is always a melancholy satisfaction in paying a just tribute to the memory of departed worth. In such case, it requires no external or formal symbols of woe to give expression to the feelings of the heart. General sympathy denotes the universal bereavement. A great and a good man has gone from among us; a mighty intellect has returned to the Divinity from whence it sprang. All that death could destroy of Thomas Ewing has been deposited in the silent resting-place of the grave! A whole nation mourns his loss! The loss of great public benefactors, in any of the departments of life, is always a national calamity. But there is a protracted period in human life, fixed by the unchangeable laws of the Almighty, when man, having performed his allotted task, stands upon the verge of time, and is ready to sink into the grave full of years and full of honors. The separation which a grateful and appreciative people mourn is deprived of half its sorrow by the reflection that his days of vigorous and active life were gone. Extreme old age, which threatens to dissolve the relations existing between the individual and the people, signalized by mutual benefits and affection, bears with it in the course of nature infirmities that impair and restrain the enterprise of man. Living as an octogenarian, he is but the monument of power and usefulness; but the grave, which encloses his inanimate body, cannot cover his bright example to excite the emulation of his more youthful survivors; and his unsullied name is still preserved to command the respect of succeeding generations. But even at such an age, private lamentation is but the echo of the public sorrow; and the bosoms which throb for the loss of a parent or a friend only sympathize with the grief and beat in unison with the stricken hearts of a whole people.

I may say with the utmost propriety, on the present occasion, that this is neither the time nor the place to enter into an elaborate study of the character and public services of Mr. Ewing. That must be postponed for more deliberate consideration, by other and abler hands, and from a wholly different standpoint. All we are called upon to do here now is to express our sorrow in this national bereavement; and that sad duty has already been very aptly performed in the resolutions so feelingly presented by the gentleman who is made the father of the Lancaster Bar by the very bereavement which we are now commemorating. It will require time, and thought, and labor to present a full estimate of the character of Mr. Ewing in all the completeness and symmetry of its moral, intellectual, and professional proportions. It will demand the highest qualities of the lawyer, and the most comprehensive intelligence of the statesman, to perform that duty. It is a fact, may it please your Honor, which will be readily acknowledged everywhere and by everybody that Mr. Ewing was a man of such rare natural endowments, and possessed of such an admirable equation of moral and intellectual powers, as would have placed him, in any age or country, in the front rank of professional eminence.

He owed this harmony between his moral and mental character somewhat to the times and circumstances of his early life—so admirably grouped together by one of his most intimate friends, a few days ago, in the columns of the daily press. The peculiar state of the country during the days of his boyhood, which had scarcely emerged from the hardships of a new and half-peopled condition, while it excluded the luxuries, the advantages and refinements of civilized life, had a strong tendency to train up the youth in those habits of simplicity and privation, of personal independence, and of constant activity of mind and body, which, however much we may shut our eyes to the fact, constituted the most essential part of the education which formed the heroes and patriots of republican antiquity.

In this state of society was Mr. Ewing's character first formed, and the early and manly impressions of his youth may be traced through the whole uniform tenor of his pub-

19

lic and private life, which stands as an enduring record of
the highest integrity and purest virtue. As a lawyer, we
feel proud of his fame. In some points he was, perhaps,
unequalled. So varied and extensive was his knowledge
of the business and affairs of life that no lawyer of his
time was a greater master of facts in cases where the
evidence before the jury was complex and contradictory.
He persuaded the minds of his auditors, whether judge
or jury, without using any of the arts of persuasion. He
convinced without condescending to solicit conviction.
No practitioner at the bar was freer from the ordinary
arts of professional *finesse*, or less inclined to appeal to
popular passion and prejudice. Nothing could elude the
acuteness and force of his logic, or the searching astute-
ness of his great powers of investigation. Whether he
displayed his powers in the forum or the Senate-chamber, I might say, in the language of another, "He opened
his arguments in a progressive order, erecting each successive position upon some other, whose solid mass he
had already established on an immovable foundation, till
at last the superstructure seemed, by its height and pon-
derous proportions, to bid defiance to the assaults of
human ingenuity." No man had greater self-reliance, or
possessed a more imperious self-will. It was this remarkable characteristic which, perhaps, more than any other
leading quality of his mind, made Mr. Ewing to be mis-
understood by a large portion of the people with whom
he came in contact, and especially among his political
colleagues and professional brethren. What they often

supposed to be an exertion of mere arbitrary will was quite as likely to be only an earnest, and sometimes, where great interests or duties were involved, an inexorable conviction of right, after mature deliberation and examination of the subject-matter in hand. With such a motive power to put into action his intellectual machinery, he strode to his object like a giant, and overwhelmed his antagonist with the weight and power of his assault. Thus stimulated, his reasoning and argumentative powers were of the highest order. For clear, masculine, and massive thought he was certainly the peer of any of the great men by whom he was surrounded, whether at the bar or in the halls of legislation.

It cannot be claimed, and I do not claim for him, that he combined all the rare elements of the most gifted oratory; but for strong natural sagacity, penetrating acuteness; for comprehensiveness, if not a quickness of apprehension, clearness, and force of understanding, against which the most subtle sophistry set itself up in vain; in situations where difficulties of the most involved and complicated character equally in vain opposed his industry and courage, he was undoubtedly one of the foremost men of his generation. He, perhaps, preferred to overcome his antagonist more by the weight of his blows than the suavity of his manner. The battle-axe of Richard fitted more readily to his hand than the cimeter of Saladin. In the battle of professional life, he relied more upon strength than policy to achieve the victory. He always brought to the management of his case, whether before this tribunal or the highest one in the land, all the forces of his wonderful mental organization ; because an earnest zeal for the interests of his client knew no difference between a subordinate and a supreme jurisdiction.   His flow of argument, in a proper case to call out his powers, whether in the court of Common Pleas or in the Supreme Court of the United States, was like a mighty stream, quickening and fertilizing everything in its swelling course.

"But no further seek his merits to disclose."

They stand confessed and recognized everywhere within the orbit of a reputation which is national, if not cosmopolitan.   The death of no man, out of public life, since the demise of Mr. Webster and Mr. Clay, in 1852, has created so profound a sensation in the popular mind in all sections of the country.   And now, may it please your Honor, I cannot, so far as my own feelings are concerned, more fittingly close this brief and feeble tribute to departed greatness, made at the request of that bar which was the theatre of Mr. Ewing's first efforts, than in the language of Mr. Justice Story, on a similar occasion, when he said: "I rejoice to have lived in the same age with him, and to have been permitted to hear his eloquence, and to be instructed by his wisdom.   I mourn that my country has lost a patriot without fear or reproach.   The glory which has settled on his tomb will not be easily obscured ; and if it shall grow dim in the lapse of time, I trust that some faithful historian will preserve the character of his mind in pages that can perish only with the language in which it is written."

REMARKS OF HON. C. D. MARTIN.

After Hon. P. Van Trump had spoken, Hon. C. D. Martin then said:

May it please your Honor:

I yield to the suggestion of the Committee, and, on behalf of the junior members of the Bar, join in a funeral tribute to the memory of Thomas Ewing. In their name, and with reverential solemnity, I lay a glove on his bier.

In my judgment, it would not be appropriate, nor is it expected of me, to sketch his biography, or dwell at length upon the prominent events of his life and career. I propose to advert in general terms, and briefly, to his character and the nature and extent of his attainments.

Mr. Ewing was especially distinct from the general class of men, and possessed physical and intellectual characteristics of the most commanding order. It matters not who were nor whence came his ancestry. His own distinction and renown could neither be enhanced nor abated by such considerations. Considered as a states-·man, a lawyer, and a scholar, he was justly eminent. Many years ago, he attained the foremost rank of distinction. He was a "Conscript Father" at a time when the title was an honor indeed; and the political history.

of the country attests his ability, learning, and eloquence in the Senate, and his great executive capacity in the Cabinet. His scholarship was of the profoundest character. He was master of the entire range of natural sciences. He was perfectly familiar with the classics, and had the keenest appreciation of the beautiful in letters.

His career, ending at the ripe age of eighty-two, is to the young a lesson and an inspiration. His manly struggles with the difficulties of early life, with the inconveniences and disadvantages of a frontier settlement, and his triumph over them all, together with his subsequent long life of eminent usefulness and distinguished honor, are known to all.

It is likewise well known, and let it be remembered, that, in addition to his commanding talents and vast acquirements, he possessed those sterling traits of character that gave him the stamp of true nobility. Temperance, veracity, courage, and honor, indispensable marks of a true man, were bright jewels that illuminated his pathway, and were treasured by him beyond all price.

To other hands than mine should be allotted the task of sketching his portraiture as a lawyer; and I shall not attempt it. The vast resources he gathered from other fields of knowledge were conspicuously useful in the practice of his profession. His arguments, distinguished by the severest logic, are, nevertheless, radiant with a glory that shows that true classic taste presided in their preparation. Many of his impromptu addresses to the jury will be long remembered as inimitable models, illustrating his superb mastery in the elucidation of complicated cases of fact. And frequently on such occasions, when thoroughly aroused, he would illuminate the discussion with the flashes of true oratorical genius. No man was more conversant with the strict forms and technical refinements, the settled maxims and artificial proceedings, of the law. Yet these, so powerful in the hands of a practised lawyer, were not his only nor his chief instrumentalities.

He moved on a more exalted plane. He explored the reason and philosophy of the rule, and enforced the claims of justice by the deductions of an inexorable logic. The science of the law has been compared to a grand temple, and the highest honor awarded to the votary who was fortunate enough to cross its threshold and behold its vast compartments. Ewing was familiar with the entire edifice "from turret to foundation-stone." He had traversed its spacious halls. He had explored its labyrinthian recesses. He was both guest and host under its high dôme. He was not an admiring occupant only; he was more—he had attained the rare dignity of architect and builder.

In recurring to Mr. Ewing's more celebrated efforts at the bar, if I may be allowed to venture an opinion, it is that his argument in the Methodist Church case is the proudest monument to his ability and genius. But the memorials of his intellectual exertions are numerous.

They are massive, grand, imposing. They will endure.

The statue, the bust, the medal ; what are they ? Cold
and inanimate. Time touches them, and they are un-
sightly. Time presses them in his rude grasp, and they
are gone. But the trophies that uncommon intellect and
learning leave to mankind are for ever alive with sacred
fire, and survive the accidents of time. They appeal to
the admiration and command the homage of successive
generations. .

And, brethren of the bar, long years after we are for
ever silent, and the very names of most, if not all, of us
are forgotten, the fame of Thomas Ewing will abide in
his works to interest and instruct his fellow-men.

The practical lesson of the hour, especially to the
junior members of the bar, is to profit by his bright
example ; to imitate his habits of study and investigation,
and, above all, his pure and spotless life.

The full measure of years was his; his the full
measure of care, and toil, and happiness, and honors. His
massive brow and commanding person will be seen of
men no more. He is gone. Gone are the proud impulses
of his noble nature. He is at rest. His temples are
crowned with immortality of glory and honor reserved
by the Father of us all for the pure in heart.

REMARKS OF WILLIAM P. CREED, ESQ.

May it please your Honor :

After listening to the eloquent eulogiums of gentlemen

who have spoken, it would perhaps be better I should remain silent; for I can add nothing to what has been said.

The beautiful tributes, so full of truth and pathos, so graphic of the great abilities, great qualities and virtues of the great dead, embodied in the resolutions of the honorable chairman and remarks of my distinguished friends, are but fitting testimonials of the regard the people of this county and members of this Bar have for the great and good man whose death we mourn, and memory now honor.

To tell you that a great man has gone from earth— one who, in an eminent degree, possessed those rare intellectual powers which made him peer of the giant minds of the land—is but to repeat that which you have already heard. All here are familiar with the life and character of Thomas Ewing. We knew him well; he was our neighbor, and at the Bar of this county laid broad and deep the foundation of a name and fame, not limited by county or State lines, but co-extensive with the Union.

How instructive his life, and what an example for emulation ! With no fortuitous aids, no powerful family alliances, but a will indomitable and a courage that could not be crushed or broken, favored with an intellect God-like, self-made, and self-sustained, Thomas Ewing rose one of the master-minds of the period, and, whether in the forum or Senate, was the recognized equal of the intellectual giants of the nation.

20

Mr. Ewing was not only great as a jurist, and eminent as a statesman, but in almost every branch of knowledge had few equals, perhaps no superior.

Well do I remember in early life, while a senator, a conversation he had in Lancaster with one equally distinguished—Mr. Browne, of Philadelphia, a lawyer of eminence, and of great scientific attainments. It was in regard to the geological formation of the Hocking Valley. Mr. Ewing's knowledge of the subject was profound, and made manifest that he was as familiar with natural history or science as the law. Both were strongly impressed with the importance of having it brought to the attention of the Legislature, that such legislation might be had as would tend to the development of its vast mineral resources. Shortly thereafter, it was done, and to Thomas Ewing, more, perhaps, than any other are the people of Ohio indebted for the early development of the hidden treasures of the State.

It is fitting and proper, therefore, that we, his neighbors and friends, the members of this Bar, where his early struggles commenced, culminating in renown, should thus publicly recognize his claims to our regard, and that the records of this Court in coming years should show how highly were appreciated the great talents, profound learning, virtues, and worth of the honored dead. He rests from his labors, and his works survive; and, while the grass grows green over the grave where he sleeps, his memory will live in the hearts of his countrymen.

REMARKS OF JUDGE SILAS H. WRIGHT.

The resolutions of the Bar and the address of Mr. Hunter are ordered to be entered upon the Journal of this Court and spread upon the final Record.

I know full well that the worm will waste this Journal and run riot with this Record; that the registry of decrees and judgments is doomed, by the nature and constitution of things, to pass away ; and that this frail memorial to the " old man eloquent" must eventually be mixed with the commonest order of the Court. And were these same orders of the Court cut in tablets of marble or engraven upon brass, time, with a kind of cruel cunning, would wipe them away and mock us with our frailty. But to-day at least is ours; and we come to signify our poor appreciation, in the last way left to us, of the great and good man whose demise has draped with sorrow the standard of every State in the Union.

It falls to the lot of few to be so mighty and so mourned. Nature seems stingy of her gifts. Her creative power is satisfied with common men. There is no planet in the skies so bright as to be seen from all the latitudes; few trees between the two oceans that overtop and outgirth the many millions, that stand the peculiar monarchs of their native mountain. Few peaks catch the first gleam of the sun. Nature is exceedingly democratic in her appointments, and careful in her designs. The world is full of little men; the skies are sprinkled with little stars; the earth is covered with small trees; hills and hillocks without number give variety to the view and a serene repose which comes from a common brotherhood. But for this arrangement, among the mountains there would be no Chimborazo, among the stars no Jupiter, among the trees no royal lords, and among the men no Ewing. Men are only great by comparison, and, when placed in a row, you may draw a line that will fairly mark their intellectual altitudes. The great ones are at dim distances, both in point of time and place. Fix the great men of the last century thus, and Ewing outmeasures them all. We are not generally fond of great things, nor is there much need of them in the small affairs of this life. We break the frowning mass of rock into fragments fit for our puny hands; we divide the river into streams, and scatter the fountain into spray; the huge oak is split into many subdivisions, and becomes manageable in human hands. Great men are the quarries out of which temples are built; they are the fountains that furnish supplies when the streams are dry; they are vicegerents of God, and utter his decrees; they permit no questioning, and rarely allow approach; and, even among themselves, they stand as distant as high mountains, and as far apart as mighty rivers. The man who wields a sceptre rarely succeeds in rocking a cradle. Even when he croons a sonnet there is the rumbling of thunder. Ewing was great in mind as he was in person. He stood high up above the measure that showed the size of common men, and the belt that clasped him counted many feet. His hat was

so capacious that it would have fallen to the shoulders
of most men, and covered them like a tent. Wherever
he went, into whatever city or strange place, all asked,
" Who's that ? " and there was always some one able to
answer the enquiry, so universally. was he known and
admired.   He had little, except a philosophical sympathy with the individual, and that was enough ; for he
had no time to squander his affection—it was measured
out for mankind.

I have known him by sight since I was ten years old ;
and nineteen years ago, when I was a law student in the
office of Hon. P. Van Trump, I spent an evening at his
house. With rustic promptness, I came at the appointed
hour, and, as none had "gathered there," he kindly
engaged me in conversation. He was so bland and
fatherly, I thought I could safely have pressed his great
hand, fashioned at furnaces and furrowed with early toil.
He said something of me which came to my ears on the
next day, and that something has been to me a stronger
stay in the battle of life than all things else together.   I
have not always been in sympathy with this great man.
We have not agreed in matters of public moment and of
great concern ; but to his superior judgment and unquestioned integrity I probably should have submitted myself.   But I could not.   His death came not with the
silent approach of a thief at night, but with full warning,
and in the day season.   The cold messenger did not
steal upon him unawares.   That would have been no
triumph.   It was a warfare of eighty odd years, and the

sunlight must stand in evidence of the struggle. On a
clear day, when no cloud was perceptible, has been heard
a clap of thunder; in the still noontide, some forest tree
falls; so comes upon us the report of Ewing's death. He
was a half century old when I first saw him, and "dry
antiquity" had scarcely disturbed a lock of his curly
hair. I have since seen his diminished form and his
crop of hair growing thinner in the harvests of time; and
the ghostly reaper has gathered and garnered him in the
great storehouse of the hereafter.

Let us say—for we may well and honestly say—as
Tacitus did of Agricola, "Whatever in Ewing was the
object of our love, of our admiration, remains and will
remain in the minds of men, transmitted in the records
of fame through an eternity of years." For while many
great personages of antiquity will be involved in a common oblivion with the mean and inglorious, Ewing shall
survive, represented and consigned to future ages.

LANCASTER, O., January 27, 1872.

HON. P. B. EWING:

MY DEAR SIR: I did not until this morning, at
Columbus, receive from the Clerk of the Supreme
Court the enclosed certified copy of the record of the
proceedings of the members of the bar, communicated
to the Court, commemorative of their estimation of
your honorable father; and as Chairman of the Com-

mittee, and in obedience to the directions of the
meeting of the bar on that occasion, I herewith trans-
mit it to you, and, through you, to the family.

With considerations of esteem and respectful regards,

Your very obedient servant,

H. H. HUNTER.

SUPREME COURT OF THE STATE OF OHIO.

DECEMBER TERM, 1871.

Hon. H. H. Hunter, chairman of a meeting held
by the members of the bar, to consider the death of
Hon. Thomas Ewing, appeared in open court, and
presented the following, which is ordered to be spread
upon the records of this Court:

*To [the Honorable the Supreme Court of the State of
Ohio :*

On the 26th day of October last, Thomas Ewing
died at his home in Lancaster, at the ripe age of
eighty-two years. He was, take him all in all, the
most distinguished man that the Ohio bar has produced—a great lawyer and great man in an age of
great men. The members of the bar feel that it is
due to the living as well as the dead that they shall
bear their solemn testimony to the value of the life
and services of this illustrious citizen, to be spread
upon the records of this court, which he dignified and
adorned by many of the choicest labors of his life.

As a lawyer, Mr. Ewing was thoroughly grounded

in legal principles; his reading was large and accurate, and he had, among other things, mastered at an early day the science of special pleading, without which no man can be an accomplished lawyer in this country or in England. He was a man of large attainments in many departments of study. In science, in general literature, especially poetry, and in history, his reading was extensive and thorough, and his memory was so tenacious that the acquisitions of a lifetime seemed to be always at his disposal.

He had great powers of analysis, great force and closeness of logic, a wide range of illustration; and while he lacked the minuter graces of style and scholarship, he had a thorough knowledge and command of the English tongue. A marked peculiarity, in which his greatness as a reasoner, like that of his contemporary, Webster, especially showed itself, was a faculty of logical statement, embodying the whole argument in the statement of his case. His genius was eminently suggestive, setting other minds to work, and thus making his presence felt in every circle, however high or humble, in which he moved.

He was a bold practitioner at the bar, relying, perhaps, sometimes too much upon a single blow in disposing of a case; and in this respect his method was in striking contrast with that of many of the leading lawyers of his day. The labor of minute preparation and care for detail were distasteful to him, and for these he relied, at all events for many years, upon the younger men associated with him; but his judgment upon the steps to be taken in the preparation of a case, and upon the case itself when prepared, was almost unerring, and in the presentation of a case to either court or jury he had few equals and no superiors, at the bar of either State or nation.

The deep foundations of his strength were laid in hard study, untiring industry, indomitable energy, unflinching integrity and honor.

Let young men who would aspire to a greatness like his seek, first, to be like him in these humble qualities. In this and no other way can the bar maintain its place in the confidence of the American people. Mr. Ewing was a man of warm and generous heart, of most affectionate and genial spirit among his family friends, full of kindness and sympathy. The struggles of his early life had undoubtedly left their traces, and given something like a tinge of sternness to his manner, and a habit of self-reliance so pronounced and unmistakable as to seem to those who only met him officially like coldness and selfish isolation. But these were only appearances, and upon the surface; while at heart he was a living and true man, and the friend and companion of good men.

The time has not yet come for passing judgment upon his statesmanship in his efforts in behalf of the Union which he loved; but we know that, whether right or wrong, he was always the *patriot statesman*, too great to be a partisan leader, too much of a man to be an intriguer or a demagogue. His leadership was one of

21

thought, of character, of life; and his influence was felt
for good in his day and generation, not only in the State
whose counsels he honored, but throughout the nation,
whose best interests, alike in the Senate, the Cabinet,
and as a private citizen, he had always at heart and
sought to serve.

The generation that knew Mr. Ewing personally will
soon have passed away, but his memory will survive; for
he has built for himself an enduring monument in the
political and legal history of the nation, and his statue
will adorn the Capitol, while his labors and example will
be felt throughout all the coming generations of the
State that he so faithfully loved and served.

Resolved, As an expression of the deep reverence of
the bar of Ohio for the memory of Thomas Ewing,
that the Supreme Court of the State be requested by
the Chairman of this meeting to place upon its records
the foregoing minute and these resolutions; and that a
copy of the same be sent to the family of Mr. Ewing,
and furnished to the press for publication; and that
Messrs. M. A. Daugherty, Attorney-General Pond, and
L. J. Critchfield be a Committee, who shall, in behalf
of the bar of the State, procure a marble bust of Mr.
Ewing, to be placed, with the approval of the Court, in
the audience-room of the Supreme Court; and that said
Committee be authorized, through sub-committees in the
several counties, or otherwise, to provide the means for
this object.

And resolved further, That said Committee be requested, in such manner as they shall deem best, to call the attention of the General Assembly, now in session, to the provisions of the second section of the act of Congress of July 2, 1864, inviting each and all the States to provide and furnish statues, in marble or bronze, not exceeding two in number for each State, of deceased persons who have been citizens thereof, and illustrious for their historic renown, or from their distinguished civic or military services, such as each State shall determine to be worthy of this national commemoration; and providing that such statues, when so furnished, shall be placed in the Capitol of the United States; and that said committee, by memorial or otherwise, ask the General Assembly to provide, by a special act or resolution, that whenever the State shall take action pursuant to said act of Congress to furnish statues as contemplated thereby, one of the same shall be that of our deceased fellow-citizen, Thomas Ewing.

THE STATE OF OHIO, CITY OF COLUMBUS, ss.

SUPREME COURT OF OHIO.

I, Rodney Foos, Clerk of the Supreme Court of the State of Ohio, do hereby certify that the foregoing is truly taken and correctly copied from the records of said court.

In witness whereof, I have hereunto subscribed my name and affixed the seal of said Supreme Court this 15th day of January, A.D. 1872.

L.S.

RODNEY FOOS, *Clerk.*

ADDRESS OF JUDGE W. JOHNSON

Before the Bar of Columbus.

The life and death of a distinguished man is an impressive lesson, and ought to be both conned and recited by the living; and those who have known him best should not hesitate to speak of those characteristics worthy to be imitated by the survivors.

In the summer of 1838, thirty-three years ago, I had the honor to preside at a public dinner given to Mr. Ewing by the young men of Carroll County, Ohio, and I had him for my guest on that occasion. He was then in the prime and vigor of manhood; and he impressed himself on my mind as the most remarkable man of my acquaintance. I have known him intimately ever since, and received from him marks of kindness and lessons of wisdom worth far more than anything I can now say of him. Of course, I am not wholly ignorant of his life.

He was not, either by birth or education, a product of the Orient. He was born on the western slope of Virginia, in that part known familiarly as the Pan-handle, in 1789, and at three years old was carried by his parents into Ohio, and planted in the wilderness.

In 1803, in conversation with Jeremiah Morrow and Manasseh Cutter, Mr. Jefferson expressed regret that the new constitution of Ohio had excluded slavery, because, in his opinion, the heavy forests of Ohio could not be cleared out by free labor. Such a blunder for so wise a man! I have sometimes thought that wrestling with the giant oaks and hickories of these forests imparted a strength and toughness, both to the bodies and minds of the boys of that period, not to be met with under what the world calls happier auspices. Such seems to have been the effect produced on Mr. Ewing, at least. His family were settled in the wilderness, without what are now called the comforts of life, doomed to hard work, few books, and no schools. His elder sister taught him the art of reading, and with this key of knowledge in his hand, in the intervals of hard labor, and at night by the light of hickory-bark, he exhausted all the stores of knowledge within his reach till he was twenty years old. A little school, dignified with the name of the "Ohio University," was about being established at "New Athens," in his own county, where some Latin, and Greek, and mathematics, and what not might be learned; but this great boy had no money and no one to help him. He laid his axe on his shoulder, and crossed over the Ohio to the Kanawha salt-works, cut cord-wood and boiled salt for two or three years, saving by the most rigid economy all his earnings, and came home—ready to enter college? Not yet; he had a higher duty yet to discharge. His father and family were struggling for life on a new farm, unimproved and not yet paid for; and laying the first commandment with promise to his conscience, and his hand on his little purse, he first cleared his father's farm of debt, and with what was left went to school.

How could so grand a beginning ever fail? That
" the hand of the diligent maketh rich," had grown into
a proverb in the time of Solomon; and the success of
the youth who renders due regard to his father and his
mother had been guaranteed by the code of Mount
Horeb. If anybody calls it superstition, so let them;
I never argue about morals or religion; but my father
taught me when a child—and to his observation of
seventy-two years I have added my own—that every
youth who commences life regardless of this duty is,
sooner or later, found to come to grief.

When his funds were exhausted, he resumed his
axe and returned to the salt-works, and cut cord-wood
and boiled salt till he had acquired enough to finish
his collegiate course; and, in 1815, the Ohio University
had the honor of conferring upon him the degree of
Bachelor of Arts—the first parchment of the kind
ever issued by that school.

I have heard Col. Armstrong, of Kentucky, describe
the return of this wood-chopper to college. The college boys, physically " but grasshoppers in his sight,"
gathered about him to make sport of him, and to
insist at recess on making a ball-alley against his
broad shoulders, taking care always not to provoke
him to anger. This sport did well enough for a while,
and he took it good-naturedly; but, in less than six
months, the students in mathematics came to him to have
him solve their problems, and the students in Latin to
have him help them out with their lessons; and he

towered up in the midst of them an object of admiration and esteem—not less their superior in mind than in body.

Mr. Ewing studied the law in the town of Lancaster, Ohio. Here he commenced his professional career, here he lived, and here he died. But his professional labors extended far beyond the circle in which he lived. I remember very well, when I was young in the profession, and willing to learn something from older men, having travelled on horseback nearly thirty miles, while our late friend, Edwin M. Stanton, travelled double that distance, to witness the gigantic struggle between him and Andrew W. Loomis in an important and exciting trial in New Philadelphia.

But I will not speak in this presence of his accomplishments as a lawyer. The thoroughness of his legal training, the singular clearness of his conceptions, his remarkable power of statement, the bold simplicity of his style, and the massive strength of his logic, are familiar to this court.

But his general scholarship outside of his profession deserves respectful notice, for he was not a mere lawyer. As a linguist, he never travelled beyond the Latin and French. These he continued to read, by way of beguiling the tedium of his winter evenings, as long as he lived. But he always bore in mind, as Dr. Johnson would say, that *words* were but the daughters of earth, while *things* were the sons of heaven. And with him the knowledge of one dozen things by

their right names was far more important than the
knowledge of one dozen names for the same thing.
Hence, his mind was devoted more to science than to
literature. His knowledge of history and general literature was far above mediocrity; but in matters of
science he was the most cyclopædic scholar I have
ever known. I first made his acquaintance, as I have
said, at a public dinner; after the public doings of
the day were over, I conducted him across the com-
mons to a little cottage I had built with a Grecian
portico in front. He laid his hand on one of the
columns, and, casting a glance up to the entablature
and the pediment, enquired, "Who did this?" I replied that I was the architect and builder both. He
paid it a compliment which it scarcely deserved, and
immediately ran into a disquisition on architecture that
would have astonished Sir Christopher Wren. He
traced the science from Egypt up to Greece, and Greece
over to Rome. He was familiar with the massive ruins
of Baalbec and Palmyra, and what not; but what astonished me was that he was not only acquainted with the
general history of architecture, but that he knew the
exact proportions of every member of each order, as if
it had been the business of his life. My business for the
day, as I had supposed, was to entertain a politician;
but I soon found that the better part of it was to be
entertained by a savant. In thirty-three years' acquaintance which followed, I never found him ignorant of any
matter of science on which I had occasion to speak to

him; and many a time I invented the occasion when there was none, to enjoy at once the instruction he gave and the charms of his conversation.

But what was most remarkable in the wide range of his scientific knowledge was his knowledge of common things. It was said of Burke that he could enter any workshop in London, and in conversation pass himself off for a brother of the craft. Mr. Ewing might have done the same thing but for the danger that his massive Doric head might have betrayed him. Part of this vast store of knowledge he used in the line of his profession; but a greater part of it was stored up and kept, because he loved it merely. What a happy thing, when age comes on, and the five senses grow dull, and the perceptive faculties begin to fail, to have on hand such a store of knowledge for the mind to feed upon; to keep the heart young and the spirits bright through the otherwise cheerless darkness of old age!

In the active developments of Mr. Ewing's life and character, he was more of a jurist than a statesman, and more of a statesman than a politician. He served one term and a half in the Senate of the United States, and he was a member of two different Cabinets. In the short time he served in official capacities, he worked laboriously, and did his work well. But, alas! for the public, it is hard to keep a man long in office, unless he is a politician; and he was no politician in the common sense of the word. He stood high above all the tricks by which politicians use and abuse their friends, outwit their enemies, and circumvent their rivals. Of course, he had little to expect from conventions; and then, he was defective in the art of winning the hearts of the masses. He recognized the brotherhood of mankind, and would defend their rights with bull-dog pertinacity; but he lacked the suavity of the spaniel. To do men acts of justice and benevolence satisfied his ideas of duty, without promises to do more, or boasts of what was already done.

But he had one quality which politicians would do well to cultivate—he knew when his time was out, and accepted the situation without complaint. He could do what no other man of my acquaintance ever could—he could retire from politics, and fall back with success on his profession. And then, a man so wise, so instructive, and so cordial by the fireside, though he might not hold the places of public trust and honor, was able to command "that which should accompany old age, as honor, reverence, and troops of friends"—worth more to an honest heart than all the shows and shams which surround men in power and place.

Though jurisprudence and science occupied Mr. Ewing's mind chiefly, he had his playthings whereby he relaxed his mind and relieved it from toil. I once, in the city of Columbus, seeing a light in his room at eleven o'clock at night, intruded myself upon him, and found him reading a little novel. "What have you there?" said I. "A love-tale," said he. "I have been working all day on a brief, and have not finished it; and if I go to bed with that on my brain, I shall sleep none; and so I have taken up this little story by way of dissipation, in order to get some rest, and be ready for to-morrow's work."

In Mr. Ewing's character, honesty could scarcely be called a virtue. It resulted from the normal structure of his mind, which, like one of those well-adjusted machines in our mints and workshops, could not do false work without first breaking or deranging the machinery. All crooked ways were abhorrent to him, and he would go straight forward, even at the cost of harshness, rather than be agreeable at the expense of truth. His early life had taught him self-reliance; and, although no man listened more patiently or respectfully to the opinions of others, I do not believe he ever relinquished an opinion of his own once deliberately formed.

I have said that our departed friend commenced life right. The first of his earnings was devoted to the service of his parents. This was his interpretation of the divine precept, "Honor thy father and thy mother." His true perception of the obligations of man to his fellow never forsook him. Next to his father, the men who helped him up by their countenance, aid, and advice were Philemon Beecher and Judge Sherman, of Lancaster. He commemorated his gratitude to the

former by naming his eldest son after him, and can-
celled his obligations to the latter by sending his son
Tecumseh to the military academy at West Point.   He
never was accused of turning the cold shoulder upon
a friend.   He was successful in business, and left a
large estate to his children; but the legacy he left
to the poor young men of the country, struggling for
wisdom, and worth, and eminence, and success, is
infinitely greater.

And now he is gone to his reward in a good old
age, leaving us to moralize upon the event.   Let us not,
then, regard this as a calamity.   For my own part,
as one whose friendship for the deceased was never
questioned, I think he had lived long enough.   He
had lived twelve years beyond the ordinary period
allotted to man.   He had accomplished his destiny
with honor both to himself and his country.   He had
lived to see his children and his children's children
growing up in happiness and respectability.   He
was approaching a time when earth could have no
charms for him; and may we not rather reckon it as
one of his blessings that he was permitted to with-
draw to his better home before the infirmities of age
should mar the beauties of a well-spent life?

[Cincinnati Commercial.]

DEATH OF THOMAS EWING, SEN.

The death of Hon. Thomas Ewing, Sen., was announced in the United States Court yesterday afternoon at five o'clock, by Colonel C. W. Moulton, who stated that he did not think the occasion a proper one for pronouncing a eulogy on the character of the deceased. He presumed Judge Swing and members of the bar would consider it fitting to take formal action in reference to this event at some future time.

Judge Swing stated that of course the members of the Bar of this city would not allow an occasion of this kind to pass without making some public declaration of their esteem for the high character and distinguished services of Mr. Ewing. In his remarks, Judge Swing also stated that when Daniel Webster died, Mr. Ewing was thought the only man able to take his place before the Bar of the Supreme Court of the United States. He supposed that the Bar of Cincinnati would be prepared to take formal action in this matter upon the reassembling of Court this morning, as the death of so great and so good a man should not pass unnoticed. The Court then adjourned.

The funeral of Mr. Ewing will take place at Lancaster, Ohio, at eleven o'clock A.M. on Saturday, and we understand that members of the bar, who desire

to be present, can reach there by way of the Little
Miami Railroad, by leaving on the four-o'clock P.M.
train to-day.

THE DEATH OF THE HON. THOMAS EWING.

Meeting of the Bar of Ohio.

ADDRESSES BY HON. BELLAMY STORER, HON. A. F. PERRY,
HON. HENRY STANBERY, JUDGE H. C. WHITMAN, JUDGE
WARDEN, JUDGE CARTER, NATHANIEL WRIGHT, AND
OTHERS.

The members of the Hamilton County Bar, and
distinguished lawyers from other parts of the State of
Ohio, some whose professional reputation extend over
the Union, assembled yesterday in the United States
Court-room, in this city, to offer an appropriate tribute
of respect to the memory of their venerable and dis-
tinguished brother in the profession, the Hon. Thomas
Ewing.   Among those present were the Hon. E. F.
Noyes, Governor of Ohio; A. F. Perry, member of
Congress for the First District; Judge Swing, of the
United States Court; Judges Storer and Taft, of the
Superior Court of Cincinnati; Judge Este, Nathaniel
Wright, and the majority of the leading members of
the Cincinnati Bar.

On motion of T. D. Lincoln, Judge Este was called
to the chair, and, on motion of Warner M. Bateman,
Judge Charles Fox was appointed Secretary

Judge Whitman rose and said that on behalf of a committee of the Bar, heretofore appointed, he desired to present to the consideration of the meeting the resolutions which had been prepared. They are as follows:

"The Hon. Thomas Ewing, at the venerable age of eighty-two, has passed away from among us. He died full of years and honor, a great man and a great lawyer. He had occupied high public stations in the Senate and the Cabinet; and in a day of intellectual giants, he was recognized a worthy compeer of all.

"The profession mourns its ablest member, its acknowledged leader; while he stood at the head of the Ohio Bar, his legal reputation was also national.

"He added new lustre to the noble science of the law by the skill, power, and integrity he displayed in its development and application. He was bold, vigorous, and comprehensive in thought and expression. He seized the strong points of a case as by intuition, and in marshalling complicated facts, before either court or jury, he was not excelled even by Webster. His intellect was massive and robust; his power of analysis extraordinary; his reading, both professional and general, large and accurate; his perceptions rapid; his memory wonderful; his industry untiring; his energy, both physical and mental, intense. His legal learning embraced all the branches of the science ; he was equally ready and able, whether dealing with the broader questions of international law or equity, or the most recondite and subtle points of real-estate learning or special pleading.   He carried into his practice, at all times, the strictest integrity, the highest honor, and the utmost fidelity to truth.   He scorned all low and cunning arts and devices, and nothing more moved his indignation than any departure in the profession from truth and honor.   He has left to his brethren of the bar a splendid legal and forensic record.

"But sweeter and more glorious than that intellectual record is the higher, better one of his private virtues and character.   Austere in morals, stern in patriotism, a lover and doer of justice, faithful in all his duties as a citizen, a friend and defender of the poor and oppressed, fearing no one, however high, despising no one, however lowly, genial in word and manner—this was known to all his friends.

"But he shone best and brightest in his own home.   Here he laid aside the severity of science, and was winning, gentle, and loving as a child.   He was friend as well as husband and father in his household, and all its members loved him almost to idolatry.

"In his death, our profession has lost its chief ornament, the State its greatest citizen.   It well becomes us to do honor to his memory—'*Esto perpetua.*'

"*Resolved,* That a copy of these resolutions, attested

by the President and Secretary of this meeting, be sent to his family, and also published in the papers of the State.

"*Resolved*, That the United States Court be requested to spread them upon its journal."

Mr. Stanbery moved the adoption of the resolutions.

General McLean seconded the motion.

REMARKS OF THE HON. BELLAMY STORER.

Judge Storer then rose and said: Mr. Ewing came to the bar one year before I was admitted; he was my senior in age seven or eight years; but, so far as the practice of our profession was concerned, we are almost equal in point of time. I knew him well, although we were separated by distance between the points of our residence. More than fifty years ago, I first made his acquaintance. I have practised with him in the Supreme Court of the United States. Two years of my life were spent at Washington; he in the Senate, and I in the Lower House. I have had opportunities on committees to confer with him on points connected with our national history and our national character and honor. We separated nearly forty years ago in public life. He afterward was called to the position of Secretary of the Treasury and Secretary of the Interior; and so far as any intimate acquaintance is concerned after that period, there

23

was but little between us. But I have always entertained the highest regard for his honor, his legal integrity, and his profound knowledge, not merely connected
with his profession, but on many questions of science.
The literature of the day was always mastered by
him, at least that portion of it worthy of being read
or remembered. He had a nice sense, as was well
remarked, of justice—justice that was formed on deep
convictions of right, not on any temporary rule of
practice or standard that meets us in the ordinary
course of life, but on that elevated ground where a
man's conscience, enlightened as his was, becomes the
arbiter of his conduct.

But, sir, why speak of a man whom all have
honored, respected, and admired? The language of
these resolutions contains all that may be said, and all
that need be said, and all that there is any necessity
for commending more particularly to the attention
and remembrance of those who have heard them
to-day. This event teaches us all what shadows we
are, and what shadows we pursue. We are reminded
that this world is one of discipline, one of continual
effort, one that is not a blank unless it is made so
by ourselves. Thank heaven! there is no blank here
in the biography. It may be said of him, "*Nulla
dies sine linea.*" He improved every minute of his
time. I never knew a man more industrious, more
methodical in all his legal pursuits, more desirous
to understand the subjects he brought his mind to

grasp, until his perceptions were as clear as a crystal. He should be remembered by those who are still young in the profession as one to whose example they may recur with profit and with pleasure, alike honorable to themselves and to his memory. Sir, you and I and my venerable brother who sits here (Mr. Nathaniel Wright), and who it affords me so much pleasure to see here, are left among the few who remember the departed in his comparative youth. We have been spared to a period that few are permitted in the order of Providence to attain. What we have done is known to that Providence—our errors, our infirmities; and whatever has been profitable to our fellow-men, if any good has been accomplished by us in the profession, if we have vindicated the law of humanity, which is but the law of the Almighty, those who knew us best, when our bodies have been committed to the earth, will be able to testify to our brethren. But you and I, sir, wish no monument of brass or stone; we wish only to be remembered by those who shall have charity for our failings, and who have the deep conviction that, in whatever position or office of importance we were permitted to hold, our great anxiety was to perform our duty, leaving the rest to Him before whom we must all appear. Let us remember that Thomas Ewing lived, but not in vain; that he died, but still lives for our example and our study.

The Hon. Henry Stanbery then addressed the meeting:

Mr. Chairman and Brethren of the Bar:

I am but just returned from Lancaster, from assisting at the last sad tribute to the memory of a friend—our deceased brother. I did not arrive in time to see my friend once more alive, but it was not too late to see that well-remembered face, cold, pale, solemn, with no answering look of recognition, which I never missed before in my life. There, Mr. Chairman, in that beautiful town he has made so famous; there, in that old homestead where he enjoyed all the happiness that belongs to domestic life; there, surrounded by every child that was ever born to him; there, with every duty of life fulfilled and accomplished, he passed from earth, and from there his body was taken to that neighboring cemetery, where, by the side of that wife he loved so well, I saw him laid quietly away. I feel in no condition, Mr. President, to speak of Mr. Ewing as he deserves to be spoken of—as a lawyer and a member of the bar. It is the man and the friend I miss now. My mind reverts to an early time, and to Mr. Ewing as he was almost a half a century ago. I remember well that day I was admitted to the bar of the Supreme Court in Gallipolis. He was on the committee that examined me. Ah! what a circle of men there were at that time on that committee, and on the bench of that court—Burnett, Heath, Goddard, King (the all-accomplished), Douglas, Putnam, and Ewing! When did the bar or bench see such an array as that?—and now the last of them is gone. Having finished their business in the court, Mr. Ewing, my friend Goddard, and myself started away together on horseback. Well do I recollect that morning in May! Mr. Ewing's point of destination was Lancaster, ours Zanesville. As we rode along, oppressed by the heat, we passed a grove of tempting shade. Mr. Ewing, quoting from the first Bucolic the lines addressed to Tityrus, invited us to repose in the shade. There it was he invited me to come to Lancaster, travel with him through the circuit, and become acquainted with the practice. I was not slow to accept the invitation. In less than a week, I was in Lancaster, and from that time for a period of fully seven years, I studied with him in his office, rode with him on his circuit—a large one—following with willing but all unequal footsteps his great leadership, witnessing his noble efforts at the bar, and learning from him what it is that makes a lawyer. It seems to me I can see him now as he was then. I first knew him in May, 1824, then in his thirty-fifth year, a man marked with a grand physical organization, such as is rarely seen united to such mental powers as he possessed. Age had not yet impressed any traces of its advance. He stood fully six feet high, well developed, possessing great physical powers, swift-footed, matchless in the race, first in all athletic exercises—such a man physically as one rarely looks upon. Yet it was not that which was so much the attraction as that fine, intellectual face, that head well poised upon his ample shoulders. One could see in looking at the physical man that he endured a life of early labor; but what was rarely seen in such a life was its combination with such a head and such a face. I have seen many men work their way up through labor and early toil into intellectual life, but never have known one whose face showed so little of the early impress of time and mere labor. It was all over intellectual, and at any time he might have sat as a study for a sculptor or a painter.

It was in these seven years, from 1824 to 1831, before he entered political life, and when his great powers and forensic abilities were all in full play, Mr. Ewing was to be seen to the greatest advantage. I confess I missed something of that fire when he left the bar for political life. I shall never forget him as he was from the age of thirty-five to forty-two, though from that day to this we must regard him as one of the greatest men of the nation. I may say that, with one exception, and that is Webster, I know of none in whom I could recognize more ability and forensic power than in Ewing. Among his chief qualities was his ability in discussing questions of fact before a jury. Though able to discuss any question before a court, it seems to me his grandest efforts were as an advocate before a jury. Of all the men I have ever listened to, he was the greatest master of facts.

When he entered political life, our relations, though not so close, continued. He was often engaged in the Supreme Court, where I met him frequently with Wirt, Lee, Webster, Choate, Davis, and the two Johnsons, and our own Doddridge and Hammond, among the greatest lawyers that we ever had. Among these he took his place in the foremost rank, second to none, as a great lawyer, save Webster alone. How these two names are associated in my recollection! Nothing could be more delightful than to hear their ordinary conversation, when the lawyers sat around, a listening and attentive audience. One day, Ewing was absent, and, on his coming in the next day, Webster said: " Ewing, you were not here yesterday," and then he quoted from that beautiful elegy he loved so well the verse commencing :

" One morning I missed him from the accustomed hill."

I shall never forget that scene, or the pathos and beauty with which Webster repeated these words.

There are many that did not understand Ewing in his character as a man. Great as he was as a lawyer, his private, domestic, friendly traits, his moral nature, attracted me even more. Never was there a more affectionate son, never a more devoted husband, never a more loving father. Some have supposed, seeing him in fits of abstraction, that he was forbidding and repulsive. My friends, there never was a more loving nature than his. With a heart as tender as a woman's, I have seen that manly face time and again suffused with tears.

He was liberal, all-embracing in his friendship, never deserting a friend. That was the character of the man, and no one feels or can feel his loss more as a friend than I do; for, Mr. Chairman, if I have at all learned what must go to make up a lawyer, if I have attained to any success at the bar, whatever it may be, I owe more to the teaching and example of Thomas Ewing than to any man, living or dead. I feel that there is a debt of gratitude on me I cannot discharge, and I shall always with great pleasure avail myself of the opportunity, whenever it offers, to speak of him as a lawyer, and of the lesson he has set to the younger brethren. Of all things in the way of preparation for the bar—I do not speak of moral qualifications—but of all other things his example taught me, was a thorough preparation of my case. O my friends! I found the advantage and necessity of it when I came to contend with him in forensic discussion. Then all that saved me were the weapons he put into my hands, the armor with which he encased me. His life affords a study for all of us, but it is to the young, the ambitious lawyer who intends to work his way up, the lesson must be of most interest.

REMARKS OF THE HON. A. F. PERRY.

Mr. Perry next addressed the meeting as follows:

Mr. Chairman: The figure which has disappeared from our bar was a grand one, and, once seen, cannot be easily forgotten. The intellectual character of the man was conspicuous and powerful. He was a great man and a great lawyer. It is not desirable on this occasion to rehearse with particularity the incidents of a long life, so much observed by his countrymen. If at any place reached by his fame, or before any audience of Americans, it would be needful to tell what he has done, assuredly that place is not in Ohio, nor that audience an assemblage of Ohio lawyers.

There was published in a newspaper many years ago a biographical sketch of the earlier part of the life of Mr. Ewing. It set forth in detail, and with a degree of fulness which I have not seen in any other production, the circumstances of his father's family and the incidents of Mr. Ewing's boyhood. I do not know who wrote it, but it was recognized by Mr. Ewing as correct. I have not lately seen the article in its original form, but I think that a biographical sketch published in one of our city papers since the death of Mr. Ewing was made up of a copy of that article, with additions relating to his later life.

The biography of Mr. Ewing, published in the *New American Cyclopædia*, so far as it related to his earlier life, was abbreviated from that newspaper article. But the incidents of his official career were carefully collated from public documents and from the debates of Congress. The space allowed for it by the publishers required the utmost condensation, and permitted little more than the merest abstract of events and dates. But it

covered the most active part of his career, and included
all his official services, with one doubtful exception.
The volume containing this article was published in
1859. In 1861, Mr. Ewing was a member of that
assemblage known as the Peace Conference.

The Conference was invited by the State of Virginia.
The members from Ohio were appointed by the Governor
of the State, and Mr. Ewing was one of them. The
gravity of the occasion, and the public interest centred
upon it at the time, were such that his service there may
perhaps be accounted part of his official career, though
the Conference had no authority or sanction in any constitution, State or Federal, and its proceedings were
abortive. His part in that conference, as in most other
transactions shared by him, was conspicuous. A committee composed of one member from each State, selected
by the Commissioners, as they were called, of the States,
was constituted, with authority to consider all proposi-
tions for the adjustment of existing difficulties between
States, and to report " what they may deem right, necessary, and proper to restore harmony and preserve the
Union." Mr. Ewing was chosen by his colleagues from
Ohio as the Ohio member of that committee. The Conference sat twenty-three days, during which time its
labors engaged the anxious and almost undivided
attention of the country. It recommended a series of
amendments to the Constitution of the United States,
which were subsequently considered by Congress, in connection with other projects for avoiding a civil war.

But the time had gone by for such conciliations, and war followed.

With the exception of Mr. Ewing's service at this Conference, the biographical sketch in the *Cyclopædia* covers his entire official career, and was recognized by Mr. Ewing as correct. The newspaper article, and the article in the *Cyclopædia* to which I have referred, form the basis for all the published sketches which I have seen. Some of the newspaper articles published since his death continue the narrative, with an appearance of authenticity, to the time of his death.

The main works of Mr. Ewing's life were at the bar. His fame was spread abroad and his great capacity made more widely known by his public official positions. But his grade as a man of intelligence was definitely that of his grade at the bar. His first official position was that of Senator of the United States, to which he was elected at the age of forty-two. He served one term, and returned to the bar. At about the age of fifty-two, he became Secretary of the Treasury, under President Harrison. After about six months, he retired from office, and returned to the bar. At about the age of fifty-nine he was placed in the Cabinet of President Taylor, as Secretary of the Interior. At about the age of sixty, he was again elected to the Senate to fill an unexpired term, having about a year to serve, after which he returned again to the bar. His whole official life occupied less than nine years.

He took his place in the Senate in 1831, one of the

last years of the Administration of President Jackson.
His position was gained and held without the help of
Government patronage; for the party with which he
acted was in a minority.   Afterwards, when he was made
Secretary of the Treasury, under President Harrison,
and still later, when made Secretary of the Department
of the Interior, under President Taylor, the same thing
was true.   The successes of his party were victories
gained by main strength, not only without, but against,
the influence of patronage.   The high positions awarded
him were due alone to his character and abilities.

When he entered the Senate, Ohio did not hold the
same relative position in the public councils which she
holds now, but was regarded rather as a frontier State.
Mr. Webster, on constitutional law and questions of
finance, occupied, without a peer, the whole field of
debate.   In the political organization of the party, Mr.
Clay was fast anchored in an unquestioned and unap-
proachable ascendency.   But Mr. Ewing made himself
promptly felt.   If I should describe here the rapidity
and strength with which he grasped the controlling
themes of the time, a true description would seem like
an exaggeration.   One has need to trace him through
those volumes of animated, sometimes acrimonious
debates to measure his enormous vitality.   Although
in a minority, it was chiefly his exertions which forced
a reorganization of the Post-office Department and of
the General Land Office.   I do not mean merely a
change of persons, but a reconstruction of the laws

which related to those important branches of the Government. To enumerate his services during those six years would be to trace the leading incidents in the history of the Senate during that time. He spoke upon the Specie Circular, upon the removal of the deposits from the United States banks, upon the tariff, upon the Force Bill. His speeches were alive with power. In a word, he commanded the respectful attention and deference of an audience accustomed to listen to Calhoun, Clay, and Webster. In that one term, he achieved a national reputation, and fixed his grade as one of the strong men of the United States.

But who does not know that the field-days of the Senate are play compared with the contests of the bar?

The first time I saw Mr. Ewing was in the Supreme Court of Ohio, at its December term for 1838. His Senatorial term had expired. The case was the Bank of Chillicothe *vs.* Swayne and others, reported in 8 O. R. 258. The last case in which I remember to have seen him was the McMicken will case, in this Court. More than twenty years intervened, during all which time, and before and after, he was distinguished for substantially the same qualities, and ranked at the head of the bar. I do not mean by this that his professional employments were more numerous or successful than the employments of some others, nor that there were not others whose services, even in a great and difficult case, might be as valuable to clients; but I mean that the qualities by which he was distinguished were great qualities, and would not permit that at the Ohio bar, or the bar of the Supreme Court of the United States, or at the English bar, his grade should be thought of as inferior to any other. He would have taken possession of the sight and thoughts of men, and become a central figure anywhere. Almost a giant in stature, well formed, with head and features of classic mould, his mind and body were fitted to each other. Direct and unconventional in manner, plain in attire as in speech, his movements of body and mind had an impetus suggestive of power to render obstructions futile. In the Senate as at the bar, he always struck directly, and with main force, for the key of the situation. There was not always absent something of the unconscious air of a conqueror. An opponent in debate had need of self-reliance and a steady balance of the nervous system; not that Mr. Ewing was rude or otherwise unpleasant in debate, but because, aside from intellectual processes and legal knowledge, his presence carried with it an undefinable ascendency of will or character.

He was a lover of literature and an extensive general reader. In conversation, he was fond of playful anecdotes and literary allusions. But in speech his thought moved to its aim with too grand an impetus to wait for ornamentation. He had the faculty of labor which habitually explored for the whole reach and bottom of his subject. I am not aware that I have ever met a stronger man. In logical power and breadth of thought, he was not inferior to Mr. Webster. In Mr. Webster's mind, imagination was a more prominent feature than in Mr. Ewing's, and I think the artistic faculty, as seen in the construction and ornamentation of his speeches, was more in use with Mr. Webster.

But for breadth, impetus, and logical force, Mr. Ewing's mind had no superior, at least none which has come within the range of my observation. At a critical and trying period in his political fortunes, I had reason to suppose myself in his confidence, and had free conferences with him. The circumstances were vexatious, and difficulties too great to be overcome. But I never heard him suggest the use of unfair or unmanly means. It may be that the necessary struggles of his early years fixed upon him an aspect of sternness which he carried through the vigor of his life. It may be that consciousness of intellectual strength became the law of his existence. His nature was too large and full not to be moved by genuine sympathies; but it was sometimes possible to wish them more demonstrative. In his latter years, after his combats were ended, all this was changed. A more lovable, affectionate, sympathetic nature was never bestowed on man or woman. As he neared the evening horizon, the orb of his being seemed to grow larger; its rays neither penetrated nor scorched any more, but filled the scene with tranquil affections. At the short session of the Forty-second Congress, held last spring, pending a debate said to have been unprecedented, he appeared on the floor of the House, supported

by a friend, and was seated for a time. As he surveyed
the actors there, his features kindled with the wonted
play of his great faculties. His presence was majestic
and venerable. He will not appear in that House any
more, nor in the Senate, nor in the Cabinet, nor at the
bar.

. While arguing in this Court the McMicken will case,
he used an expression, considerately muffled, which could
mean nothing else than negation of religious belief. It
did not imply positive disbelief, but simple absence of
belief. With such a mind as his, the line between
religious belief and the want of it is narrow. It depends
upon the existence of Deity and immortality of the soul,
and belief in those is less the result of reason than of
intuition; rather a part of the constitution of the mind
than a product of the mental operations. It would seem
that as his will, the dominating trait of his mental
structure, subordinated itself to the supremacy of his
affections, he left that side of the line on which he stood
at the McMicken argument, and passed over to the side
where stood his departed companions at the bar, Goddard, Wilcox, Hitchcock, McLean; where also waited for
him the departed mother of his children.

REMARKS OF NATHANIEL WRIGHT.

Mr. Nathaniel Wright said he wished to make a few
remarks, more particularly in regard to the character of
Mr. Ewing. It was very noble and very lovely. It is
not much, even in these degenerate days, to say of a man

that he was upright, just, firm in principle, faithful in duty, steadfast as a rock in what he believed to be right. These were traits which every lawyer should possess; but there was something peculiar, something gentle and genial about his nature that threw a charm over his character, and attracted everybody to him. He was thrown, in the latter days of his life, into positions which provoke not unfrequently the sarcasms and bitter vengeance of party spirit; but it is remarkable that, if we look over the newspapers of that day, we do not find in any of the popular declarations or harangues anything of personal bitter abuse. His friends who differed with him believed he was an upright, conscientious man, whom everybody must respect; and outside of that circle over the nation at large there was a kind of atmosphere of character pertaining to him that pervaded the whole nation—a general sentiment of respect toward the principles, character, and conduct of the man. His character was to be studied, especially by the members of the bar. True worth in his case reaped its reward in this world, and surely will in a better one.

REMARKS OF HON. A. G. W. CARTER.

Mr. President and Brothers of the Bar:

> "The death of those distinguished by their station,
> But by their virtue more, awakes the mind
> To solemn dread, and strikes a saddening awe:
> Not that we grieve for them, but for ourselves,
> Left to the toil of life."

We of his brethren "left to the toil of life," who are

23

assembled here this day to give due respect and honor
to the memory of the departed Thomas Ewing, are not
called upon to grieve or lament, but rather to rejoice in
the memory of the great traits of character of the
deceased, and to thank Heaven that his life was so long
and so useful, and that he has arisen to a higher sphere
of existence, in which his life is continued to accomplish
far greater and better results than when clogged by the
material grossness of this earthly being. We rejoice to
know that he who has departed was distinguished by his
station, but by his *virtue* more; and although our minds
have been awakened to solemn dread, and struck with
saddening awe, it is not that we grieve for him, but for
ourselves. We meet together to do honor to the excellence of his life for the sake of the living, and not for the
dead. We who survive here convene together to manifest to the world that we shall keep in sacred memory,
and respect, and love, and affection what was great and
good of our departed brother, and hold it ever close and
dear in our minds and hearts, that we may be the better
for it, and, in our lives here, may be enabled to accomplish more good and use for the benefit of humanity.

" Wise judges are we of each other."

From the very nature of ourselves and our existence, it
is quite impossible for any one of us to sit in judgment
upon another. No one can judge us properly and truly
but He who seeth all things. We come not to judge of
Mr. Ewing! We come to do honor to those noble traits

of his conduct of life which were so apparent that all who ever knew him or had his acquaintance might readily see. We judge not, that we be not judged; and what we shall say of Mr. Ewing shall not be in the spirit of judgment, but in the spirit of praise and laudation, for high and great qualities of mind and heart, which certainly and eminently belonged to him. His death does not grieve us; he lived long, and nobly, and full of honors. We deplore not his death; for

" All that live must die,
Passing through nature to eternity."

But we rejoice in his great, exemplary life, and are glad to know that in such a world as this there was such a man and such a life!

I remember that, while I was yet a youth at college, the name of Thomas Ewing as a lawyer and a statesman stood foremost among the great sons of Ohio. He had then achieved the lofty position of Senator from Ohio in the Senate of the United States, and as such was high in rank among the then great names of the Senate. His name was frequently associated with those of Clay and Webster, and the people of Ohio of all parties felt proud of his name and his standing. His first service as United States Senator was from the year 1831 to 1837; when retiring from the strife of political life, he returned to his peaceful home in Lancaster, and resumed his practice of the law. This was Mr. Ewing's first political position—that of a Senator of the United States. It is

given to but a few of our fellow-citizens to achieve at
the start in public life so high a position. Mr. Ewing
before this—from the year 1816, when he was admitted
to the bar of this State—had been practising law with
distinguished success in the courts of the State and of
the United States, and from his position as an eminent
lawyer was at once transferred to a seat in the national
Senate. He had not been a hackneyed, ambitious politician, a seeker for place and office, but, honored for his
political wisdom, he was considered a great statesman,
and the Whig party of that day, without action or solici-
tation upon his part, placed him in high, honorable position; and, when he was once so placed, he did honor to
his State and the nation, acquiring for himself at once
a national reputation equal almost to that of any senator
in the Union.

In the year 1841, on the accession of President Harrison, Mr. Ewing was appointed Secretary of the Treasury,
which office he held until September of that year, when,
with other members of President Harrison's cabinet, he
resigned his office, unwilling to follow the fortunes of
the administration of John Tyler, who had succeeded
to the Presidency on the demise of General Harrison.
Again Mr. Ewing retired to private life, and again resumed the practice of the law. When General Taylor
was made President, in 1849, Mr. Ewing was again
called to the councils of the nation, and he organized
the newly-created Department of the Interior, having
been appointed the Secretary. In 1850, after the demise

of General Taylor, Mr. Ewing resigned his office as
Secretary of the Interior, and was appointed by the
Governor of Ohio once more to the United States
Senate, to fill the unexpired term of Mr. Corwin, who
had been appointed Secretary of the Treasury by President Fillmore. He served as Senator until the year
1851, when, his term of office having expired, he once
more gave up public employment, and betook himself
to the practice of the law. No more do we hear of him
in public station until the year 1861, when, the great
civil war threatening, the Governor of our State, because
of his great fitness, appointed Mr. Ewing as a Peace
Commissioner in the ill-starred National Peace Conference called together by the State of Virginia. This
Peace Convention, as all know, was an utter failure;
and Mr. Ewing, now in declining age, gave up public
position entirely. But during the war of the great
Rebellion, he was by no means still, in his private station. Having done all he could to stay the bloody and
unholy work in the beginning, his voice and pen were
nobly on the side of the Union when the cry was,
"Havoc, and let loose the dogs of war!" And when,
too, the cruel war was over, Mr. Ewing, from his private
place and peaceful home, was again ready, in his true-
born patriotism, to counsel his countrymen to forget and
forgive, and thus more strongly and thoroughly perpetuate the bonds of union, and restore the peace and
happiness of his countrymen and the glory of his
nation.

This, then, is a brief epitome of the public services of our distinguished departed friend. In his life, though perhaps often, he was not long in office; but when in office, he was the true patriot and the true statesman. He was always for his country, and, without any selfish consideration, his duties he performed for the good of the people. I never belonged to the same political party as did Mr. Ewing—being always, until of late years, of the opposite party in politics—but I have this to say of Mr. Ewing, that I never saw aught in him of political guile or machination. Indeed, I never looked upon him as a mere politician. In public character, he was always to me a statesman, and as such I viewed him. Personally, of late years, coming sometimes in contact with him and getting well acquainted with him, my opinion of him as a statesman and a true patriot was greatly confirmed. I remember a conversation I had with him just at the close of the war of the Rebellion, when the uppermost question was what was to be done with the States lately in rebellion, and his significant reply was, "They must be treated as Territories, and, at the proper time, must be readmitted into the Union." This was the first time that I had heard that idea suggested; and, even at this late day, it frequently occurs to me, particularly in consideration of all that has happened since, that it would have been the wisest and surest plan of reconstructing the Union. In his subdued age and latter life, Mr. Ewing, with all his faculties about him, was still the patriot and statesman. He had lived a long life as such, and as such he died, when—

> " He gave his honors to the world again,
> His blessed part to heaven, and slept in peace."

But, brethren of the bar, it particularly concerns us to speak of our honored friend as a lawyer. It was in the profession of the law that he was especially one of us— our brother. There are some of venerable years among us at that time, who were associated and intimate with Mr. Ewing in professional relations, and one of these has addressed us in feeling and eloquent terms. But most of us have been personally little acquainted with Mr. Ewing as a lawyer at the bar, though all of us well know his great reputation; and that reputation speaks to us in most unmistakable terms that Mr. Ewing was the leading lawyer of our State, if not of the nation. It was my fortune, when upon the bench of the Common Pleas and District Courts of this county, to see and know Mr. Ewing as a practising lawyer. He argued several cases before me and my associates, and I must be permitted to say, as extensive as I knew the reputation of Mr. Ewing to be, his great and high standing as a lawyer was more than confirmed in my opinion, when, as a Judge of the Court, I was permitted to see and know his ability and learning. I remember well his conduct of a very important case in the District Court. He had as colleague and adversary two of the most prominent lawyers of the bar of Ohio. In the argument of the case before the Court, his colleague and adversary consumed some six or seven hours of time. Mr. Ewing, taking the chief points and principles of the case, and which comprehended all there was of law and fact involved in the case, in a terse, strong, and forensically eloquent argument, consumed only about three-quarters of an hour of the time of the Court. I mention this one instance of the practice of Mr. Ewing, because, as I am informed, it illustrates all. Mr. Ewing, fully comprehending and grasping the great legal principles and the sum of the facts of the case, argued briefly and tersely upon them alone, and let the small niceties and legal quibbles and technicalities to those who cared for them. He confided in the justice of his cause, founded upon the real legal principles and the facts involved, and hurled these at the mind of the Court with all necessary power and discretion. When he was afloat upon his case, he pursued the wide and deep stream of it, unmindful of the small tributaries, which he left for others to pursue as they might think fit. It was this extended, comprehensive power of Mr. Ewing that made him a truly great lawyer, and gave him that unwonted success at the bar. He was indeed a natural lawyer, and, because of that, his mind was eminently judicial; and often have I thought that it would have been well for his country had Mr. Ewing occupied the place of Chief-Justice of the United States. He was emphatically fit for that high office!

It is not needful to say more of Mr. Ewing as a jurist,

as, in what has been said, we have comprehended his real and genuine greatness as such; and it would be well for us all, as lawyers, to keep in mind that the greatness of Mr. Ewing, as a lawyer was not in his learning and experience in the cases or the technicalities of the law, but in the profound principles, reason, and justice of the law. He was a man emphatically of justice in the law, and to his legal mind all else had to succumb. During his long career of practice at the bar—much over a half-century—it never could be said of him:

> " In vain thy reason finer webs shall draw,
>   Entangle justice in her net of law,
>   And right, too rigid, harden into wrong;
>   Still for the strong too weak, the weak too strong."

It becomes now my pleasing duty to speak of our distinguished brother as a *man* among his fellows; and here it is that his character, ever above reproach, stands out in bold relief. All who have ever seen him full well know that he was marked with a splendid physical personality; and his surmounting, massive brow and head showed most plainly the brains within. His mental and intellectual strength were very great; and this showed itself, not only in the field of politics and jurisprudence, but in all departments of life. His mind, too, was garnished with much useful information and learning beyond that necessary in his profession and public life; and per-

haps no man was, during his whole life, a more diligent student than he. His intellectual house, of much
magnitude, he filled with every form of use and
adornment, and managed it all for the good of his
fellow-men.

Gifted so in mentality, he was by no means wanting in heart. On the contrary, to those who knew
him well, his heart was as great as his mind; and in
all his social relations as husband, father, and friend,
he was loving and beloved. Among his fellows he
moved with much dignity, and attracted much respect;
and underlying that serious and solemn aspect of person and carriage was the affection of a brother and
a friend, which attached to him with "hooks of
steel" those who knew him well. He was a man of
whom it can be truly said that, throughout his long
and useful course, he was pure, clear, and free from
guile, incorrupt, and above suspicion.

"Integer vitæ, scelerisque purus."

Such in this life was our great friend; and we do
not lament that death has stricken him down. He
has not fallen—he has arisen. His death was his
rebirth into another and a better world. It is the
divine law—birth, growth, life, decay, death, rebirth—
all progress: and Mr. Ewing has been like all of us
will be, but a subject of the law. In him the law
has been fulfilled, and he has been born again.

> "For though the soul of man
> Be got when he is made, 'tis born but then
> When man doth die; our body's as the womb,
> And, as a midwife, death directs it home."

Says the great apostle, "There is a natural body, and there is a spiritual body; and when we lay off the corruptible one, we take on the incorruptible. This is the law."

Go for a little while with me to the sculptor's studio. We are modestly and gladly welcomed, and we enter. There, among other objects of beauty, we see a remarkable statue, pointed out to us by the excellent artist. It is a statue of perfect manhood. We look and admire:

> "See what a grace is seated on this brow:
> Hyperion's curls; the front of Jove himself;
> An eye like Mars, to threaten and command;
> A station like the herald Mercury
> New-lighted on a heaven-kissing hill.
> A combination and a form, indeed,
> Where every god did seem to set his seal
> To give the world assurance of a man."

The statue, in all its startling beauty is moulded in clay—the dust of the earth. Soon the artist approaches, and, climbing to an eminence above the statue, cries out to us, "Behold! Again behold!" And with drawn and uplifted hammer, to our amazement he instantly strikes the statue, and off, off the yielding, crumbling clay falls in appalling ruins. But, lo!

lo! in its place on its pedestal stands still the statue
of manhood, in the same form, features, attitude, and
lineaments; but now, oh! how resplendent in gold—
in its shining, golden texture to stand for ever! The
earthly clay was but the coarse covering of the statue
of gold. We are struck dumb with awe! So with
our eminent friend. The great Master-Artist of the
universe, lifting the hammer of death, has but struck
off the mortal clay, and Thomas Ewing, in golden
immortality, still lives.

> "He lives in glory; and his speaking dust
> Has more of life than half its breathing mouths."

REMARKS OF JUDGE WHITMAN.

Judge H. C. Whitman said he owed an apology for
rising to address the meeting at this late hour, and
in the presence of many abler and older members of
the bar, and would have remained silent but that he
desired to express, as a comparatively younger member of the bar, the high honor and privilege he had
felt in witnessing the great intellectual efforts of Mr.
Ewing, in the enjoyment of his professional friendship
and the hospitality of his home. He felt the debt of
gratitude, and should feel it all his professional life.
He had heard in Washington the ablest members of
the bar, and was familiar somewhat with the reputation
of Mr. Ewing, but was by no means prepared for the
extraordinary displays he afterwards witnessed, filling

him, not only with astonishment, but almost with awe.
He seemed to have taken advantage of the remark of
Edmund Burke in relation to the science of the law—
that while it tended in the first instance to make the
mind more acute, unless fortified by learning, it ended
in making it narrow; for his researches, his studies,
were not limited to the mere abstract science of the
law, but he went out into every department. He was
a master of Shakespeare, of Milton, thoroughly conversant with all the English classics, familiar, too, with
the best writings of the old Romans. He went thoroughly into the domain of the natural sciences, and
as a historian, there were perhaps but two men in
this State who could be called his equals—one was
the Hon. William Allen, the other the Rev. Archbishop Purcell, the distinguishing peculiarity in each
being the extent of his historical knowledge. Without wearying this honorable meeting, he (Judge Whitman) desired simply to say, in addition to recording
in this public manner his humble tribute to the memory of Mr. Ewing, that, in his judgment, he was in
almost every branch of the law as great a lawyer as
this country ever produced; in the power of marshalling complicated facts before a court and jury, fully
the equal of Webster. His life was an example to
the young. No man can rise by genius, unless he
define genius by labor; and his genius was untiring
and methodical, never despising small things.

REMARKS OF GEORGE E. PUGH.

Mr. Pugh said, though the meeting had been prolonged beyond the ordinary time on such occasions, he could not suffer the opportunity to pass without bestowing his humble mite of admiration where so eminent a gentleman, with whom he was acquainted for more than a quarter of a century, had passed from among them. Mr. Pugh then recounted several of the cases in which he appeared with Mr. Ewing, and passed a handsome eulogy on the abilities of the great lawyer and statesman. He was a finished scholar, his conversation the charm of all who heard him, his character an honor to the profession, and, since the death of Webster, the greatest lawyer in the United States.

Judge Warden and J. L. Miner followed in a few appropriate remarks.

Judge Swing and Judge Este also paid brief but handsome tributes to the memory of the great deceased, after which the resolutions were then put from the chair and adopted.

[Cincinnati Commercial.]

THOMAS EWING.

Upon yesterday the bar of Hamilton County convened for the purpose of paying its tribute of respect to the memory of the great lawyer, who was universally acknowledged as the leader of the profession in the State of Ohio. It is very rare that a meeting of the kind has produced such a profound impression upon those who attended it, and it is also rare to find so much ability and good taste united to pronounce eulogies at once so high and so just.

It is difficult for friendship to praise without excess of commendation, and it is difficult to estimate the ability of one who has occupied position, and won applause in discharging great and honorable duties, without that natural tendency to exaggeration which may be considered, if not a failing, at least an incident, of human nature.

But the proceedings of the bar displayed a singular excellence. Eulogy was not too high wrought, and the remarks of all who spoke evinced great feeling, admiration, and respect. They illustrated the fact that the character of the deceased had impressed itself upon the hearts and minds of those who knew him in a way such as only a great and good man could.

REPORT OF THE PROCEEDINGS

IN THE

SUPREME COURT OF THE UNITED STATES

On the announcement of the Death of the
Hon. Thomas Ewing.

Although it is not a usual matter for this Court to notice in its proceedings the death of members of the bar, the venerable years of Mr. Ewing, his eminence as a lawyer, the long term, ending only with his life, in which he was constantly engaged at this bar, and the reputation which he had throughout the country, both in professional and public life, seemed to have caused a departure from the practice in his case.

Mr. Ewing was born in Ohio County, Virginia, December 28, 1789. His father, who had served in the American army during the Revolution, and had become reduced in circumstances, removed his family in 1792 to the Muskingum River, and thence to a place in what has since become Athens County, Ohio. He was here taught to read by an elder sister, and by extraordinary efforts of his own acquired a fair elementary education. At the age of nineteen, he left home, and worked in the Kanawha salt establishments, until, in the course of two or three years, he had saved money enough to enter the Ohio University, at Athens. His money being exhausted, he

returned to his salt works, saved his earnings again,
then resumed his studies, and in 1815 received the
first degree of A.B. ever granted by the Ohio University. He studied law in Lancaster, Ohio, and was
admitted to the bar in 1816, and practised with great
success in the State courts and in this Court. In
March, 1831, he took his seat in the Senate of the
United States as a member of the Whig party, and
became associated with Mr. Webster and Mr. Clay
in resisting what were deemed the encroachments of
the Executive, and in support of the Whig measures
generally. In March, 1837, his term of office having
expired, he resumed the practice of the law. Upon
the election of President Harrison, in 1841, he was
appointed Secretary of the Treasury—an office which
he retained under Mr. Tyler (who, by President Harrison's death, in one month after his inauguration,
succeeded to his office) so long as Mr. Tyler acted in
accordance with the views of the party by whose
electors he was elected. With most of the other
members of President Tyler's Cabinet, he resigned
office in September, 1841. On the election of President Taylor, in 1849, he was appointed Secretary of
the then recently created Department of the Interior,
which was still unorganized. On the death of that
President, July 9, 1850, and the accession of Mr.
Fillmore, a division in the Whig party caused a
change in the cabinet. Mr. Corwin became Secretary
of the Treasury, and Mr. Ewing was appointed by the

27

Governor of Ohio to fill the unexpired term of Mr.
Corwin in the Senate. In 1851, he retired from
public life—in which he was engaged, taking it all
together, for about nine years—and resumed the
practice of the law. However, in 1861, when the
Rebellion was imminent, he became a member of the
assemblage known as the Peace Conference. This Conference was invited by the State of Virginia. The
members of Ohio were appointed by the Governor of
that State. The Conference sat twenty-three days,
but conciliations were impossible. The South was
determined on rebellion, and the war came.

Mr. Ewing died on the 26th of October, 1871, at his
residence in Lancaster, Ohio, in the eighty-second year
of his age. His abilities were known to those of the
departed or departing generation perhaps more than to
those of the present one, although he continued to practise in this court until within a short time; the last case
which he argued having been, I think, Maguire vs.
Tyler, at December Term, 1869, which, on account of
his venerable years and imperfect strength, he was gra-
ciously requested by the Court to argue sitting. Among
the most elaborate of his written professional arguments
are those in the case of Oliver vs. Pratt et al., involving
the title of a large part of Toledo, Ohio; the case of the
Methodist Church division; the McIntire Poor-school vs.
Zanesville; and the McMicken Will case, involving large
bequests for education

On the 28th of October, after the intelligence of his

death reached Washington, a meeting of the bar of this Court was held, when, on motion of Mr. Carlisle, the Hon. B. H. Bristow, Solicitor-General, was called to the chair, and Mr. D. W. Middleton appointed Secretary. The resolutions set out below (which were drawn up and offered by Hon. T. W. Bartley, of Ohio) were unanimously passed. On the opening of the Court on Monday, the 30th, Mr. Attorney-General Akerman, in appropriate terms, announced the melancholy event which had led to them, and laid them before the Court, as follows :

" *Resolved,* That the members of the bar of the Supreme Court of the United States have received with profound sensibility the announcement of the death of the late Thomas Ewing, of Ohio, long and eminently distinguished as a jurist and statesman.

" *Resolved,* That we hold in high estimation the memory of the deceased as one of the great men of the country, illustrious for public services in the councils of the nation, and eminence and ability in the profession of the law.

" *Resolved,* That the Attorney-General of the United States be requested to communicate these resolutions to the Court, with the request that they may be entered on the record; and, further, that they be communicated to the family of the deceased, with the expression of the sympathies of the meeting."

The Chief-Justice made the following reply :

" The Court share with the bar the sentiments expressed by their resolutions, which will be entered upon the records, in accordance with their request.

"We all feel that whatever honors can be paid to the memory of Mr. Ewing are properly paid.

"His is the record of a youth patient of toil and full of aspiration; of a manhood worthily employed in various and honorable public trusts, and in forensic labors, which gave us frequent occasion to note the remarkable grasp and vigor of his intellect, and the great variety and extent of his attainments; of a protracted and serene old age; and of a calm and peaceful death, surrounded by children worthy of their father.

"To family and friends, the death of a relative and friend so honored and beloved, however long deferred, comes always too soon. Counting ourselves as not the least affectionate among the friends of Mr. Ewing, we yet find, and doubt not that all near to him in friendship or relationship will ever find, consolation in reflecting upon the brightness of the example he has left for the imitation of his countrymen." (12 Wallace.)

MEETING OF THE BAR AT ATHENS, OHIO.

At a meeting of the bar of Athens, held on the 10th day of June, A.D. 1872, the following proceedings were had upon the death of Thomas Ewing:

The committee heretofore appointed, composed of Hon. A. G. Brown, Colonel R. E. Constable, and Hon.

W. R. Golden, reported the following resolutions, which were unanimously adopted:

"1st. *Resolved,* That the Bar of Athens County, in common with others, regard the death of Hon. Thomas Ewing as a great public loss, and will cherish his memory with highest veneration.

"2d. *Resolved,* That his exalted character and attainments and his distinguished career afford an eminent and worthy example for aspiring youth and for the admiration of all.

"3d. *Resolved,* That inasmuch as it was in this county that his early days were spent and his education acquired, and his opening legal talents were for a series of years displayed and appreciated, the bar and people of Athens County claim a peculiar interest in his fame, and cannot permit the opportunity to pass without the offering of one more to the many tributes paid throughout the land to his exalted worth.

"4th. *Resolved,* That these resolutions be requested to be spread upon the minutes of the Court, and that a copy thereof be forwarded to the family of Mr. Ewing, at Lancaster."

Upon the assembling of Court, on the morning of June 10, A.D. 1872, the Court, on motion, directed the proceedings of the bar of Athens, upon the death of Hon. Thomas Ewing, to be spread upon the records of this Court.

PROCEEDINGS OF THE FACULTY OF THE OHIO UNIVERSITY.

Whereas, It has pleased ,Almighty God to remove from earth the Hon. Thomas Ewing, the first graduate of this institution, and one who was greatly distinguished both as a lawyer and as a statesman ; therefore, be it

1st. *Resolved*, By the Faculty of the Ohio University, that, by the death of Mr. Ewing, we are made sharers in a common loss; for his early connection with this institution, first as a student and afterwards as a trustee, has given her a special interest in his fame. We have observed his eminent career with grateful pride, and have felt that his elevation of character, his purity of life, his sagacity as a statesman, and his power as an orator, were an ornament and an honor to his *Alma Mater*.

2d. *Resolved*, That we commend his noble example of energy and aspiration for the imitation of those who now succeed him as students in the University.

3d. *Resolved*, That these resolutions be spread upon the records of the Faculty, and that a copy be transmitted to the family of Mr. Ewing.

A. S. GIBBONS, *Acting Pres't.*
W. H. G. ADNEY, *Secretary.*
OHIO UNIVERSITY, ATHENS, O., June 15, 1872.

MEETING OF THE ATHENIAN LITERARY SOCIETY OF THE OHIO UNIVERSITY.

Hon. Thomas Ewing departed this life a few days since in Lancaster, Ohio. He graduated in 1815, receiving the first degree given by the Ohio University—that of A.B.—when few students and fewer universities claimed a place in the new West.

Of his college career we know but little; yet we know of a truth that his difficulties were many, his conflicts were fierce; and if his life was a success, he merits the credit.

But Thomas Ewing's work is ended. His fittest monument is the institutions of our country, which he strove to perpetuate, and the inscription thereon:

"LIBERTAS ET NATALE SOLUM."

At a recent session of the Athenian Literary Society of the Ohio University the following resolutions were adopted:

"*Whereas*, This Society has heard with deep sorrow the announcement of the death of Hon. Thomas Ewing, one of its most venerable members; therefore,

"*Resolved*, That in his death we lose an honored member, and the nation sustains an irreparable loss.

"*Resolved*, That as a testimony of respect for his memory, we drape our hall in mourning for thirty days.

"*Resolved*, That these resolutions be published in

the Athens and Lancaster papers, and that a copy be
sent to the family of the deceased.

" A. B. RICHARDSON,

E. M. JACKSON,

D. C. CASTO,

" *Committee.*

" October 30, 1871."

MEETING OF THE ALUMNI OF THE OHIO UNIVERSITY.

At a meeting of the alumni of the Ohio University,
which was held in Athens, June 18, 1872, the following
action was had :

Hon. Ben. Smith, from the Committee on the death
of Hon. T. Ewing, reported as follows :

" Thomas Ewing, the first and probably the most
distinguished graduate of the Ohio University, having
departed this life since the last meeting of the alumni of
the institution, it is believed to be eminently fit and
proper that we should at our first meeting succeeding his
death express our estimation of his character, and spread
our opinions on the record of the alumni ; therefore,

" *Resolved*, 1st, That, in the opinion of the alumni of
the Ohio University, he stood among the foremost of our
country in general literature and in the varied departments of learning.

" 2d, His mental faculties were calm, reflective, and
admirably balanced, and well guarded against hasty

extremes on all subjects. His judgment was clear, and his conclusions almost faultless. All questions of importance were examined by him with calm consideration, and, when decided by him, were never yielded to popular influence or personal or political considerations.

" 3d, He never was a favorite of professional politicians, because his stern integrity and unselfish patriotism repelled the approach of all fraud, insincerity, and duplicity. His great ability, his indomitable energy, and honest patriotism, in despite of politicians, extorted from his country the eminent position he occupied in the councils of the nation.

" 4th, It is with pleasure and honest pride that we assert with truth and in all sincerity of heart that our friend and brother, after a long life of usefulness, has left us a reputation of pure moral excellence, without a blot or a single blemish."

THE PIONEERS OF ATHENS COUNTY.

[The following valued account of my father's association with the pioneers of Athens County was kindly furnished me by his long-cherished friend, Hon. A. B. Walker, himself a pioneer.—E. E. S.]

As showing the interest Mr. Ewing felt in affairs in Athens, and in matters relating to her older citizens, with whom he was intimately acquainted in his earlier years, we present from the record of the Pioneer Association the following letter from him, under date of Lancaster, July 21, 1869 :

" DEAR SIR : I have yours of the 15th instant. You may add my name to the Association, but there is little prospect of my being able to attend any of its meetings.

"I am, very respectfully,

" T. EWING.

" A. B. WALKER, Esq., *Secretary.*"

At a meeting held in Athens, July 24, 1869, we find this minute :

" The meeting directed the name of T. Ewing to be added to the list of members of the Association as a corresponding member."

At the same meeting, the name of Bishop Ames was added to its members, besides a large number of the older citizens of Athens County. At this meeting Hon. Isaac Barker presided ; he was then in his 90th year.

. On the 4th of July, 1871, the Association met at Amesville, at which place Mr. Ewing was expected to be present and deliver an address. His health was such as to prevent attendance, but he wrote and sent with his son, Gen. Thomas Ewing, Jr., a most excellent letter, which was read by Gen. C. H. Grosvenor to, and warmly received by, the Association. The letter is copied and sent with this communication. By a vote of the members, it was ordered to be copied in full upon the minutes of the Association :

"The following letter from Hon. Thomas Ewing, Lancaster, was read to the meeting by Gen. C. H. Grosvenor, of the Executive Committee, which, from its importance, is copied at length into these minutes:

"LANCASTER, July 3, 1871.

"GENTLEMEN : I find it will not be in my power to attend the Amesville Pioneer celebration on the 4th. Though my health is tolerable, I cannot endure even a small amount of fatigue, and, on consulting my physician, he advises me not to venture.

"I would be very glad to meet you all, the living friends and associates of my boyhood and early youth, and the descendants of those that are gone; but, as I cannot, I send my third son, Gen. Thomas Ewing, Jr., whom I trust you will find a creditable representative of the first pioneer.

"I visited Amesville a few weeks since, after an absence of fifty-five years, and found my memory fresh as to places and persons. The streams appeared small, and the valleys narrow, but rich and beautiful as when I last knew them. To me, while I lived in it, and until I left it, it was a happy valley; there was little material wealth in it, but it verified the assertion of the poet, that a people,

"'Though very poor, may still be very blest,'

and there can grow up no inordinate wealth here to disturb the quiet tenor of life. While it is abundantly prosperous, its tranquillity is not in danger of being destroyed by those terrible commotions which distract the greater world.

"Mr. Walker's history of Athens County marks well the calm and steady progress of this happy valley in population and in mental culture, much of which is due to our early Library Association; and I am strongly impressed with the opinion that it is entitled to one year's earlier date than his record gives it.

"In the spring of 1803, my father removed his family to a small farm seven miles southeast on the Marietta road. In this I am not mistaken, as I made record of the date on the bark of a beech-tree, which I have seen often since. I remained on the Amestown farm, to go to school and help my brother take care of the stock. Judge Walker came in November of that year, and occupied the principal cabin, and such of our family as remained a smaller one the other side of the little run. I was reading a library-book—*The Children of the Abbey*—and had got together a good supply of hickory bark to make me a light, and I rose an hour or two before day, and sat on a stool by the fire reading. Henry Bartlett, Esq., who happened with us that night, came and sat also, and asked to look at my book. I handed it to him, and, as he returned it, it fell open on the fire, and scorched and spotted several of the leaves. By the rules of the library, there was a fine for every spot, and, in counting over the injury in fips and levies, I found myself a bankrupt boy. However, I took the book to the next library meeting, explained the misfortune, and the Board very kindly remitted the fines. If the volume (I think it was the second) be still in being, it must bear the marks of the adventure.

"This antedates Mr. Walker's record several months. I think the money was raised, and the books bought and on hand, before that record was made out, and that it is but an official recognition of a past fact. As to *Morse's Geography*, I studied it as early as 1800; but it was no doubt a book on hand, afterwards turned in by Mr. Cutler and my father as part of their contribution to the library.

" I remember a rural scene of the summer of 1800, simple and childish, but illustrative of a fact in history. Mrs. Brown had a handsome little tomato-plant of the small; round kind, which was then called love-apple. It was not known among us as an article of food until several years after the French inhabitants of St. Domingo had been driven from the island and took refuge on our shores, and then its use extended slowly. On the day named, children of the two families were at play in Mrs. Brown's garden, when suddenly the alarm was raised, and ran through the little group, that Apphia Brown had eaten a love-apple. We sped with the fearful intelligence to the grown-up people, who did not partake of our alarm, and it passed off without a catastrophe. It was many years later when I first saw the tomato used on our tables as an esculent.

" For many years, we had no post-office nearer than Athens; but my father's little farm, on the Marietta

road, was passed once a week by a mail carried on horseback between Clarksburg, Virginia, and Chillicothe—
one week east, the next week west.   I always took
care to be on hand when the mail passed.   It was carried by a boy of sixteen or seventeen—John Davis—who
became my intimate friend ; and I fed his horse, and
mother gave him supper and a bed with me by the fire,
as a reward for the news he brought us.   I have often
sat up till ten o'clock listening for his horn ; he was very
punctual with his satchel of

> " ' News from all nations, lumbering at his back.' "

I am indulging in trifles, but,

> " ' Those little things are great to little man,'

and I write as I would talk with you if present.   I
wish all our assembled friends many happy returns of
this glorious day.

"I am, very respectfully, yours,

"T. EWING.

" C. H. GROSVENOR,
  L. BROWN,
  D. B. STEWART,
  THOMAS F. WILDES,
  GEORGE PUTNAM,
          "*Committee.*"

The following telegram was received on the day of
its date, and is filed :

"LANCASTER, O., October 26, 1871.

"To A. B. WALKER:

"Thomas Ewing died this P.M. Funeral Saturday, eleven o'clock.

"H. H. HUNTER."

The Secretary of the Association has very thoughtfully and wisely collected in a scrap-book articles from all the leading papers of the Hocking Valley and the State, and the press in various parts of the country, upon the death of Mr. Ewing. These extracts are prefaced as follows: ·

"Hon. Thomas Ewing died at his residence in Lancaster, O., October 26, 1871, in the eighty-second year of his age.

"Mr. Ewing was a man of national celebrity, and justly honored in life by the first in this country. He was 'Ohio's greatest and noblest son.' The deceased was a member of the Athens County Pioneer Association, by whom his memory is now cherished."

At a meeting of the Association, held in Athens, April 6, 1872, announcements were made of the death of both Messrs. Ewing and Hunter.

Remarks were made upon these announcements by Hon. John Welch, Hon. A. G. Brown, and others.

In speaking of Mr. Ewing, Judge Welch dwelt at length upon the purity of his private character, which he pronounced "without spot or blemish." He spoke also of his mind, patriotic intentions, and great experience and usefulness in public life; of the example for emulation his life affords, and the instruction to youth with which it was filled; of his profound knowledge of the law and his great power as an advocate; and, as the Secretary has well expressed in his minutes of Judge Welch's remarks, " the picture given his auditors of the beauty and grandeur of this great and excellent man in all the social and domestic relations of his life was in the highest degree interesting."

Judge Brown also spoke of Mr. Ewing, endorsing fully what had been so well said by Judge Welch, from a life-long acquaintance with the distinguished statesman.

The above is respectfully submitted by the Executive Committee of the Athens County Pioneer Association to the friends of the late Hon. Thomas Ewing, as a slight mark of the esteem in which he was held by our people, as feebly indicating the sorrow felt by us at his decease, and as a token to them that, though dead, he is not forgotten by those who knew him through all the years of his eventful and useful life.

Thos. F. Wildes,
Chas. H. Grosvenor,
Leonard Brown,
D. B. Stewart,
George Putnam,
    Executive Committee.

Athens, June 17, 1872.

REMINISCENCES FROM PAPERS.

THOMAS EWING.

THOMAS EWING is dead. The last of that galaxy of great men, who in the Augustan age of the American Senate so charmed and delighted the civilized world, has departed. Webster, Clay, Calhoun, Crittenden, Benton, and Ewing are all gone to their final rest.

Cold and dull indeed must be the heart which animates an American bosom that will not be stirred with emotion at this announcement. The name of Ewing is associated intimately with those of Webster, Clay, and Crittenden; he was the peer of the two latter, and the compeer of all of them.

In intellectual scope, power of analysis and of combining thoughts, exactitude of statement and in concentrated imagination, Mr. Webster had no equal; but in all of these qualities Mr. Ewing stood in the front rank of the second line. In penetrating the motives, quickening the impulses, and moving the hearts of men, Clay surpassed Ewing as Crittenden did in the dexterous use of the weapon at his command; but if Ewing's scimeter was not as sharp as Clay's, and if he did not wield it with the aptitude of Crittenden, his arm was stronger, and his weapon heavier, than that of either of them.

29

Webster once said of Ewing that he was the best-informed man he ever met—that he never conversed with him five minutes but that he was wiser for having done so. Ewing was a man of large physical frame, and of great physical power, and his intellectual strength was commensurate with his physical force. He was modest in his demeanor, patient in investigation, clear, able, and convincing in argument, and decided in his judgment. He seemed to those who knew him to be so open that there was in him no purpose that was concealed, and as if there was none to conceal; for to human observation he had no vices.

As a lawyer, he was industrious, learned, judicious, and careful. His practice was extensive and diversified. The decisions of the Supreme Court of the United States are enriched by his arguments, and he has long been recognized as one of the foremost men who practised before that tribunal, and as the leader of the bar "west of the mountains."

Mr. Ewing was born in Virginia, December 28, 1789. He received his early education chiefly from an elder sister.

Mr. Ewing grew up with his State. In his lifetime, Ohio, from a wilderness peopled only by Indians, has grown upon the sisterhood of States, and now takes rank but a little behind the most populous and flourishing States of the Union. How much Mr. Ewing's energy, his example, his moral worth, and his great intelligence have contributed to this result we can never know.

Though his usefulness has been extended beyond the period which has been ordinarily allotted to man, and he has been gathered at a ripe age, and when his work was done, his death will be felt as a personal loss, and he will be mourned in thousands of American homes.   S.

[Ohio State Journal.]

REMINISCENCE OF HON. THOMAS EWING.

In the allusions made to the religious opinions of Mr. Ewing at the Cincinnati bar meeting, some doubt seemed to be indicated as to what those opinions were. Since reading the proceedings of that meeting, I have hunted up Mr. Ewing's argument in the great Methodist Church case in the Circuit Court of the United States, in which I find the following passages, which seem to me so pertinent and important in their bearing upon the matter above suggested that I venture to send them for publication in the *State Journal:*

"But I may be permitted to say in conclusion that I deeply deplore the controversy between the Methodist Episcopal Church South and the Methodist Episcopal Church, and more especially the separation which is partly its cause and partly its consequence. There is a faith essentially of union and love, and the Methodist Episcopal Church, in its union and by the united efforts

of its devoted and self-sacrificing sons, has done great
and lasting good throughout our land, especially among
the masses, who have felt most and profited most by its
influence.

"The Christian religion is emphatically the philosophy
of the unlettered man. It teaches him, by the direct
speakings of revelation, what philosophy in all ages
has sought to discover and comprehend—the duty of
man to God, to himself, to his fellow-man; the mystery
of his origin, his being and condition here, and the
deeper and darker mystery of his final destiny. The
learned, in the pride of intellect, have not all and at
all times been satisfied with the teachings of revelation,
but have endeavored to advance, by force of their own
reasons, to conclusions on all the subjects on which it
has pronounced; and, failing in this, have ended by
a denial of revelation, and often by disbelief or
doubt of all things, even of their own being, because
they could not comprehend or explain them. The past
century, in which Methodism arose, witnessed their
mightiest effort and its most terrible results.

"It was not the mission of John Wesley to reason
down by force of logic the systems of false philosophy
which had usurped possession of the human intellect,
and let loose from the restraints of conscience the wild
and ferocious passions of men, but to explore the depths
of man's religious nature, and awaken and disclose to
him the perceptions and convictions of religious truths,
known to his consciousness, which the understanding

cannot fathom or reason explain. This was his distinctive philosophy, exercised and enforced by the ever-
present but sometimes slumbering consciousness, which
he sounded the tocsin to awake. Thus armed with the
gospels of life and truth, attended by this ever-present
witness, he went abroad, and he sent his sons and
followers abroad, to preach repentance, and faith, and
holiness throughout the land; and faithfully and well
has their mission thus far been fulfilled.

"I have from my earliest remembrance been familiar
with the onward movement of the Methodist Episcopal
Church, which always kept pace with the advancing
population of our Western wilds; and I have noted
well its social, moral, and civilizing influence, not only
on those brought within its pale, but beyond them
in the communities in which it took root. But all that
we have witnessed of its achievements was done in
union and by united efforts. Will it still go on after
secession and severance, unchecked, to the consummation
of its mighty mission? We know not—God knoweth."

It will be observed that this eloquent statement of
the nature and influence of the Christian religion cannot,
consistently with the well-known character of Mr. Ewing
for candor, be explained away by attributing it to the
zeal of the advocate in the discharge of professional
duty. We have here the direct affirmation that the
Christian religion teaches man—even the unlettered
man—"by the direct speaking of revelation, what philosophy in all ages has sought to discover and com-

prehend—the duty of man to God, to himself, to his
fellow-man; the mystery of his origin, his being and
condition here, and the deeper and darker mystery of
his final destiny "; and that the opposers of this religion
were the advocates of "systems of *false* philosophy,
which had usurped possession of the human intellect,
and let loose from the restraints of conscience the wild
and ferocious passions of man." And it is further
affirmed that Wesley and his followers "were armed
with the gospels of life and truth," to preach repentance,
and faith, and holiness throughout the land.

I remember very well how my heart was moved by
the eloquence and power of this statement when I first
read it, and that I ventured to say to the great and good
man who uttered these precious words that, if they
correctly stated his convictions, I hoped he would not
delay the duty of a more formal profession until, like the
great Webster, he should on his death-bed regret that
he had not said and written more on these subjects.
His answer was, "Well, I do believe all I then said in
regard to the Christian religion." T. C. J.

HON. THOMAS EWING.

EXTRACTS FROM MY SCRAP-BOOK.

To the Editor of The Leader:

The first time I saw Mr. Ewing, Sr., was when I was
a boy of nineteen years of age.

He was then in the meridian of his manhood, in active

practice in all the higher courts, both State and national, and, as a lawyer, stood confessedly as the acknowledged head of the bar in Ohio. He was in the full vigor of his powers, and his splendid physical frame was surmounted by a massive, noble head, indicating abilities of an extraordinary character. At this time, the little old brick court-house, where the Supreme Court held its sessions, was in the State-house yard at Columbus; and I well remember, as Mr. Ewing walked through the narrow hall and up the wretched, creaking staircase, he seemed to dwarf the dingy building, and make it look still smaller and more wretched than ever. When he rose to speak, every eye was fixed on his noble presence and commanding form, and the court, bar, and spectators gave him the most earnest and respectful attention.

He began his argument with apparent diffidence, and proceeded cautiously, slowly, but with great method and exactness, in stating his case. He evidently did not intend to exhaust his strength before reaching the rough points of the trial. So have I seen a noble and stately ocean steamship move with almost painstaking care and solicitude at the beginning of her voyage, seeming to have scarcely motive power enough to force her huge bulk across the smooth waters of the harbor—a mimic sea, with its bright waves and sparkling surface. But as the swell of old ocean began to be felt around her, and the great waves came rushing at her head, how grandly and powerfully did she rise to meet them! *Then* how the strength and the power came as they were needed; and with what majestic dignity and grandeur would she overcome all opposition, meeting and defying the mightiest waves, and dashing before and behind her with invincible power all opposing obstacles!

As Mr. Ewing warmed with his subject, he seemed to carry conviction to all his hearers, and poured forth, without apparent effort, his wonderful knowledge of law, science, literature, philosophy, and art—everything that could illustrate, support, or strengthen his case in the realms of learning or logic was ready to his hand; and to me, the boy of nineteen, he seemed a prodigy of learning and the greatest man I had ever known.

Mr. Ewing was a member of Congress, a Senator of the United States, a Cabinet minister, and, for nearly half a century, was in active public life. But office could add nothing to the dignity of Thomas Ewing, or advance him in any manner in the respect or good-will of the people of Ohio.

His high character, great talents, prodigious and varied learning, and commanding abilities, were everywhere acknowledged, and he will long be known and remembered as one of the foremost of American scholars, lawyers, and statesmen.

To the mass of mankind, who held no personal relations of intimacy with Mr. Ewing, he always appeared cold, austere. But I am told by those who knew him best, and who shared his confidence and regard, that this was wholly a false estimate of the man.

An old friend of his once told me that when at home,

surrounded by his family and grandchildren, it was delightful to watch this great man, as, with the most affectionate solicitude and unselfish, childlike devotion, he gave himself up to entertain, amuse, instruct, and gratify them. Here he was surrounded by those who knew and loved him, and here, like Sir Walter Scott, he was cheerful, light-hearted, vivacious, and, with his younger grandchildren, frolicsome and jocose.

His father was a Revolutionary soldier, and, becoming greatly reduced in circumstances, in 1792 settled upon what is now the town of Athens, Ohio. Thomas, a huge, bulky, vigorous boy, was taught to read by an older sister. His love of knowledge was intense and untiring. While working upon his father's farm, at the age of seventeen, he learned that twenty miles away there was a copy of Virgil; and he rode on horseback through the woods, with only a blanket for a saddle, to borrow or to buy it. He succeeded in getting the precious volume, and absolutely mastered its contents by studying during the daytime every leisure moment, and at night pursuing his labor of love by the light of a burning pine torch. At the age of twenty, he worked as a laborer in the salt-works at Kanawha, and here he was able to obtain for himself a little money to pay his expenses at college. In 1815, he graduated at the University of Athens, and received the first degree ever conferred by an Ohio College. He was admitted to practise law in the year after, and rose, as I have said, to the highest place in the profession.

30

At the time of his death, he probably had as profound a knowledge of law, the classics, history, sacred and profane, poetry, the arts and sciences, architecture, and belles-lettres as any man living; and all these vast stores of learning were classified and arranged with such consummate order and exactness in his brain that to each special professor of some branch of learning, when called upon to discuss that particular subject, he appeared as though he must have devoted the larger portion of his life to the acquisition of knowledge upon that particular subject only. He was a poet of more than ordinary excellence, and could, if occasion offered, recite for hours almost a volume of poems, which he had written and committed to memory in his earlier days.

Mr. Ewing lived during a most remarkable period of the world's history, and but little of what was passing escaped his scrutiny. His earliest home was the wild frontier; and he heard in childhood the wild howl of the wolf and the still wilder whoop of the savage, and saw the primeval forests fall under the axe of the hardy pioneer. Schools, neighborhoods, churches, colleges, and the advantages, and ways, and means of civilized life, were in his early days almost unknown to him; and the log-cabin, with its rude surroundings, were the architectural structures to which his eyes were accustomed. He was four years old when Louis XVI. and his beautiful wife, Marie Antoinette, were beheaded by the French people. He read by torchlight the stirring and brilliant speeches of the younger Pitt, who died when young Ewing was

seventeen years old.   With all the details of the history
of George III., who died as late as 1820, and his still
more profligate son, George IV., who died ten years
later, he was as familiar as with his own history.   He
welcomed Lafayette on his visit to this country, and
passed a high eulogium upon his character at his death
in 1834.   He read with glistening eyes and palpitating
heart the speech of Robert Emmet, when in 1803 he
was so illegally and unjustly condemned to death.   In
his day lived Goethe and Schiller, with whose works he
was perfectly familiar.   He watched with intense solicitude the march of events during the wonderful career of
Napoleon the Great, until it closed in a lonely death, in
1821, at St. Helena.   He survived to tell his grandchildren the story of the second French Revolution; while
in his old age he sat in his easy-chair and read the story
of Sedan and the destruction of the French Empire.   In
his day, Sir Walter Scott wrote his first and last volume
of the "Waverley Novels," and they were eagerly read
by Mr. Ewing as they came, one by one, to America.
He lived almost to witness the invention and perfection
of the steam-engine, and to see the lightning, originally
caught by Franklin, "harnessed by Professor Morse."

He saw Ohio rise from a barren wilderness to an
empire of two and one-half million souls.   He saw
slavery, permitted if not sanctioned by the Constitution, become so great that its power spread all over
the land, and dictated to Presidents, Cabinets, Courts,
and National as well as State legislatures.   He saw

it crush the spirit and degrade the manhood of four
million of our people.   He lived to the close of the
great Civil War, and saw freedom and equal rights
guaranteed by the Constitution to every human being
in our Republic.   He saw the nation, in his day, a
small and scantily settled country with thirteen States.
At the time he died, the Union consisted of thirty-six
States and forty millions of people.   Well might he
exclaim, "What wonders God hath wrought!"

His knowledge of the public men of America was
perhaps more extensive than that of any man who
has lived in our country.   Living under every administration inaugurated in the United States, and with
most of them as an active and influential friend or
opponent, his opportunities for personal acquaintances
with men were wide and various in the extreme.   He
was thirty-seven years old when Jefferson died, and
knew him, Madison, John Jay, John Marshall, William Wirt, Webster, Clay, Calhoun, Pinckney, Hayne,
the Adamses, Benton, together with nearly all the
Presidents who for fifty successive years presided over
the destinies of the Republic.

Perhaps no man who was a mere spectator took a
deeper personal interest, or felt a keener solicitude, in
the result of the late Civil War than Mr. Ewing.
Every step taken by our armies was watched by him,
and he had a broad and comprehensive knowledge of
the plans of the different campaigns, and discussed
them with the most intelligent, and sometimes astound-

ing, sagacity, as to their results. When General Sherman was attacked for what was charged upon him as a military blunder during the war, he sprang eagerly to the rescue, and with a bold and vigorous pen, and full knowledge of his subject, defended successfully General Sherman and his military action, with the same freedom and knowledge as though the science of warfare had been a study with him from his youth.

Mr. Ewing died during the close of the first administration of General Grant, and went to his grave laden with many years, surrounded by his family and friends, and taking with him to his honored rest the respect and esteem of a nation which he had served with earnest zeal, and the profound regard and friendship of all who had ever come within the scope of his influence.

REMINISCENCES OF THOMAS EWING—HIS EXCELLENCE IN ATHLETIC SPORTS.

A correspondent of the *Ohio State Journal* writes:

"I was born in the old village of Franklinton, which was the seat of justice for Franklin County until 1825 or 1826. In my boyhood, I was a frequent attendant in the old Court-house during the sessions of the Court, where was often gathered the best legal talent of the State.

"I well recollect the first time I saw Thomas Ewing, then a young lawyer, not yet having much business or making much of a mark. I was struck with his large head and generally massive and muscular but rather awkward build. It was summer-time, and the Court had adjourned early in the afternoon. Several of the lawyers remained, and the conversation turned upon athletic exercises and feats of strength. Among those present was Joe McDowell, a brother of Abram and John. He declared that he was so swift of foot that he had never been beaten in a race of one hundred yards, and he believed he could not be beaten, and offered to bet ten dollars he could beat any one in the crowd. Finally, Orris Parrish took him up, and they went out on the green. It was not yet determined who was to be McDowell's competitor; but when the ground was measured off, Mr. Ewing, who had taken but little part in the conversation, and whose demeanor had been very modest and retiring, offered himself to run the race, and to the surprise of all, for none supposed he could run. Judges and stakeholders were appointed, and I will never forget the gleam of Ewing's eye or his air of resolution as he stripped off coat, vest, and shoes, and took his place. The word 'go' was given, and the young athletes sprang off with an even start; soon, however, Ewing began to gain, and came to the winning-post well ahead of McDowell, who was so chagrined at the result that he began to find excuses, and said he had tripped and stumbled, or otherwise he would have won. Ewing smiled and said: 'Well, if you are not satisfied, let us try again.' They did run again and McDowell was beaten worse than before. Other sports and trials were made—standing-jumps, running-jumps, shouldering stones, throwing the axe and the maul—in all of which Mr. Ewing proved his superiority; and finally the high jump over a stretched string was tried. Mr. Ewing made no attempt at this, until Mr. Mc-Dowell, who proved the best, challenged him to 'beat that.' Ewing replied: 'Well, let us see your best'; and when McDowell was done, Ewing put the string four inches higher, and stepping back a few feet, came at it with a curious sidelong swing and motion, and over he went amid the cheers of the crowd.

"Some twenty years ago, when serving on the city School Board with William Long, we were one evening waiting for a quorum, when our conversation ranged over some of the men and incidents of our early settlement. Said Mr. Long: 'It was, I think, somewhere about 1814, when I was a chunk of a boy, that my father sent me in search of some horses that had strayed away. We were then living in Ross County, and I had gone up into the eastern edge of Pickaway, looking in the rich range of that region for the missing horses, when, crossing one of the natural grassy prairies, and listening for the sound of the horses' bell, which was familiar to me, I found a cow-bell in my path, which I fastened to my body, and amused my-self with its clatter as I walked along.   At some dis-tance, I perceived a man coming in a direction that would soon intercept my path. As we approached, I noticed he was dressed in a hunting-shirt and buckskin breeches, and intently reading a book. As we met, he stopped suddenly, and thrusting the book into the bosom of his shirt, he said abruptly, 'Where did you get that bell ? '   'I found it back here,' I replied. 'Well,' said he, 'it is my bell, and I mean to have it.' I replied, 'If you are stronger than I am, you can get it.' He immediately seized me with a hug like a bear, and attempted to crush me down. I was strong, active, and wiry far beyond my looks, and, after a severe tussle, he suddenly . let me go, and, breaking into a hearty laugh, said : 'You are a better man than I took you for; what is your name ? ' I replied, 'My name is William Long; what is your name ? ' 'Tom Ewing is my name,' was the reply.

"He enquired the way to the Scioto salt-works, and, after a few minutes' conversation, we parted, he pulling out his book and reading, and I rejoicing in the clatter of my cow-bell.   Our next meeting was in the Court-house in Franklinton, years afterward, where I had been summoned as a juror.

"I mention these incidents now, I trust, without impropriety; for I believe it was the early physical training which Mr. Ewing received that enabled him not only to compete successfully in all athletic sports, but gave him also that capacity of endurance that his great brain-power required. We all know what an intellectual giant he became, and that in his death Ohio has lost her foremost man, one whose memory she will cherish and delight to honor hereafter, when the mists and prejudices of parties and of politics shall have cleared away."

RECOLLECTIONS OF THOMAS EWING.

After an active campaign of the summer of 1859, having distributed over three hundred copies of my bust of Governor Chase to his friends and admirers, I returned to Columbus to engage in other commissions.

Meeting Governor Chase one day, he said: " Whom do you propose to model next?" I replied: " A bust of the Hon. Thomas Ewing." The Governor very kindly remarked: " I am happy to hear it, and wish you a decided success; for Mr. Ewing has by far the grandest head in Ohio."

While proceeding to Lancaster, just twelve years ago this month (October), over the old stage route, up hill and down dale, it is needless to say that I approached my prospective subject with more than ordinary diffidence; for it was there I was to meet a ripe scholar, a gentleman and statesman—a man that was revered by the public, and almost " time-hallowed " with age.

The weather was delightful, and the pleasure of our journey was much enhanced by the dreamlike and golden haze of the atmosphere of an October afternoon, and the infinite variety of tints and colors of the autumnal leaves, forcibly reminding me of Fosdick's beautiful poem commencing,

"When Indian summer, like an Indian queen," etc.,

which has not its peer in our language.

Descending into the Hock-Hocking Valley, it was not long before we could see in the distance the dim outlines of the city of Lancaster, and, to the left of us, the ever-welcome sight to every returning wanderer from a foreign land—the bald and rock-ribbed front of Mount Pleasant, crowned with its dwarfed and yellow pines and mountain laurels.

Arriving in Lancaster in the evening, I presented myself at the old family mansion of Mr. Ewing, where I was courteously received, and their generous hospitality tendered me during my sojourn in their beautiful city. I most gratefully thanked the Hon. Mrs. Ewing for her proffered generosity, at the same time informing her that I was an old bachelor of incorrigible habits, but, with her consent, I would remain at the Talmadge House.

"Well," said Mrs. Ewing, in a playful manner, "I presume we will have to let the old bachelor have his own way," at the same time modestly informing me that she had ordered apartments prepared for me previous to my arrival. I could only thank her again, and bless my stars for having made the acquaintance of a lady, as I subsequently learned, of innumerable Christian graces.

Mrs. Ewing was a remarkable woman, and in the heyday of youth she must have been very handsome; and, even when I saw her, there was a charming grace about her "beyond the reach of art." She was truly a worthy companion of so noble a husband, beloved by her neighbors, and adored by her family and friends.

The old family mansion was, and is yet, a two-story brick house, built on a hill. It had a broad hall in the centre, with sitting-rooms and parlors on either side. There was very little about the exterior of the antiquated residence to command admiration; but it was plain, and, like its possessor, very substantially built, and that which pleased me most was the quaint finish of the interior.

Not far from Mr. Ewing's family residence was a little brick office or study. It was there he mastered the Spanish language in a marvellously short space of time. He had a real estate case in St. Louis that involved several hundred thousand dollars. Nearly if not all of the old original records or title-deeds were written in the Spanish language.

He at once saw the great importance of a thorough knowledge of language as well as facts. He shut himself up for six weeks in his little brick study, as he himself told me, and at the end of that time he was able to go into court and translate those Spanish documents or records with the best of them, and gained his case.

I secured agreeable apartments at the Talmadge

House, where I was to receive sittings from Mr. Ewing whenever it suited his convenience, and those sittings were numerous and very far between, which gave me ample time for study and much reading of rare books furnished me by Mr. Ewing and his kind friends.

After several interviews, I found Mr. Ewing all that he had been represented, and more too; and saw before me a man of majestic form and of giant mind, whose rays of thought, like the summer's sun, were created, as it were, to enlighten and bless mankind.

Mr. Ewing reminded me more of Daniel Webster than any man I had ever met. Neither of them had any of that chit-chat about them peculiar to General Taylor, but much of the facetiousness of Corwin and the animated conversation of Henry Clay. Both Webster and Ewing were great thinkers, Miltonic in their thoughts, with all of the profundity of a Bacon.

Mr. Ewing always spoke of Henry Clay with enthusiasm, of Daniel Webster with a depth of emotional feeling. His anecdotes of Mr. Webster, and poetical quotations included, would fill a large volume; and yet there was not the least ostentation in his allusion to great men or the classics, for both had been his most intimate companions for years.

Soon after my arrival at Lancaster, I had my modelling-stand and clay set up for active labor. To make assurance doubly sure in so important a work, I first made a preparatory study of a cabinet size to ensure the proper pose for the finished model.

During Mr. Ewing's first sittings for his bust, his conversation very naturally turned upon events of his own, and the early history of Ohio, that were so graphically portrayed by an old friend of his in the *Daily Commercial* of the 27th ultimo.

Now, like old Prospero, with the magic wand of memory, I am compelled to conjure up other scenes and incidents that have not already appeared in print, at the same time, I hope, to the entertainment of your numerous readers.

About this time, Mr. Ewing left for Washington for a few weeks, and I was left at liberty to amuse myself as best I could.

On the return of Mr. Ewing from Washington, the social relations were again complete; for without his presence in Lancaster, there was a void—something was wanting—like a grand historical statue that had long been the pride, emulation, and inspiration of the residents of their beautiful city.

He was in the humor again, at our first meeting, to entertain me with anecdote and story, and events of his early experiences in the primeval forests. The *naïveté* of manner in which he told them was always delightful and instructive. Nothing seemed to have escaped his wonderful memory of persons and things, and his accumulated thoughts and suggestions were a world of his own.

He never despised the day of small things, for these were the nucleus, or nebulæ, upon which he built greater and grander structures. He had a mind to comprehend

at once the beginning and the end.   Like all great men,
if ever deceived at all, it was by himself and not by
others; for the impetuosity of genius knows no bounds,
and they alone are responsible for the result.

ᵗ I cannot avoid relating one of the many incidents of
his early experience, as told by himself: "While a party
of young people were out horseback-riding one Sunday,
and passing through a heavy-timbered forest and dense
underbrush, they heard a sudden shriek of pain and
alarm.

"The company halted, and soon learned that one of
three boys had been bitten by a rattlesnake, and the
other two were carrying him home with all possible
speed.

"My young lady friend very modestly removed one of
her garters, with which we bound up the wounded boy's
leg, to prevent too rapid a circulation or progress of the
poison.   We gave all necessary directions in such cases—
gunpowder-tea, etc.—and proceeded on our journey, and
subsequently learned that our patient was happily preserved.

"About forty years after that event, as I was returning in a carriage from Columbus to Lancaster, the weather being very warm, I stopped at a farmhouse by the
roadside to give my horses some water.   The farmer's
wife, for such she proved to be, very kindly handed me
a water-bucket, with which to help myself at the well.

"While watering my horses, I noticed that she scruti-
nized my face rather closely for a stranger, and when I

returned the water-bucket with thanks, she enquired, 'Are you not Mr. Ewing?' I answered in the affirmative. She was silent. 'But why did you ask?' 'Well, I see you have forgotten me.' 'Indeed!' 'Yes; but you cannot have forgotten the young woman that gave you the garter to tie up the rattlesnake-bitten boy's leg.' 'I do remember that incident very well. But is it possible that you are that woman?' 'Yes,' she replied, 'and I have lived on this farm almost ever since.'"

It was very natural for such a man as Mr. Ewing to indulge in the classics of his youth, and he not unfrequently alluded to Homer, Hesiod, Virgil, and Horace. Horace was one of his great favorites, for he told me he generally read him through in the original *once a year*.

Not being familiar with the originals above named, Mr. Ewing would very kindly give me a few free translations, and did it apparently with all the pleasure and enthusiasm of a youth.

With all of his love and enthusiasm of the Latin poets, he did not overlook the English classics, from old Chaucer down to Byron. The poetry of Milton and Dryden were especial favorites of his. With the *sentiments* of either he gave little heed, for he was *too much* of a well-bred gentleman for that. It was the art, the music, and the soul of the better man that received his approbation.

Milton's "L'Allegro," "Il Penseroso," and "Mask of Comus" were great favorites of his, and, for the music

and harmony of our language, he recited a passage
from Byron's "Parisina" as a fine example:

> " It is the hour when from the boughs
>   The nightingale's high note is heard;
> It is the hour when lovers' vows
>   Seem sweet in every whispered word;
> And gentle winds and waters near
> Make music to the lonely ear.
> Each flower the dews have lightly wet,
> And in the skies the stars are met,
> And on the wave is deeper blue,
> And on the leaf a browner hue,
> And in the heaven that clear obscure,
> So softly dark, and darkly pure,
> Which follows the decline of day,
> As twilight melts beneath the moon away."

Nothing could exceed his recitation of such beautiful gems, so full of pathos and feeling; and to me it
was a double pleasure, the grand subject before me,
in full play of thought and sentiment, without the
least restraint or exaggeration.

When in the humor, Athenæus, Plutarch, Montaigne,
and Cervantes came in for a full share of his admiration. One thing I liked about Mr. Ewing—he never
professed to have any knowledge of authors and books
that he had never read, and well digested, too.

No branch of science or art seemed to have escaped
his attention. One day he would indulge in all the
various theories and mysteries of geology. The next
day, perhaps, he would ascend from earth to heaven,
and give a brief but beautiful history of astronomy.

At another sitting, perchance, he would take up the subject of mechanics, and seemed to dwell with all the pleasures of an enthusiast on the intricacies and construction of all manner of steam-engines and manufactures of every description.

Like a well-bred gentleman as he was, he very rarely alluded to religion, politics, or private affairs. He was always ready to entertain, instruct, or to amuse, but never indulged in saying anything in the social circle that might give offence, and that which would be proper and much better expressed elsewhere.

I never made an allusion to poetry, or attempted a quotation, but Mr. Ewing would recite the whole passage, if necessary. His familiarity with most of our modern poets was extraordinary.

One morning, I remarked that I thought Byron had written some of the most beautiful, as well as delicate, shades of human expression of all our poets.

Said he: "Let me hear them."

> " He who hath bent him o'er the dead
> Ere the first day of death is fled—
> The first dark day of nothingness,
> The last of danger and distress
> (Before decay's effacing fingers
> Have swept the lines where beauty lingers),
> *And marked the mild, angelic air,*
> *The rapture of repose that's there* "—

" A very nice discrimination," said Mr. Ewing, and recited the balance of the paragraph, some twenty-nine lines, in his happiest manner.

Another point he had not overlooked. That was that Byron had written the most beautiful description of antique and modern sculpture of any on the subject, in ancient or modern times. It is true that old Homer, of "Scio's rocky isle," had set the example in his description of Achilles' shield, proving conclusively that the art of sculpture was in a high state of cultivation before Homer or the *Iliad*.

The British drama had many charms for him, particularly Gay's *Beggar's Opera :*

> " How happy could I be with either,
> Were t'other dear charmer away!
> But while ye thus tease me together,
> To neither a word will I say;
> But tol de rol," etc.

At times, at a single sitting of a morning, he would give me a free translation of one of Molière's plays. Molière was an especial favorite of his. Mr. Ewing was very rarely surprised by being asked a question on any given subject. One morning, I ventured to ask him whether he was acquainted or familiar with an Irish character in Shakespeare? He very promptly said, "There is no such character in Shakespeare." " Pardon me, Mr. Ewing, with all due deference to your literary lore, you will find an Irish character in *King Henry the Fifth.*" "Let me see it, sir." Taking up a volume of Shakespeare, and turning to Third Act, Scene Second, at the same time handing him the book, he read the whole of the scene between

" McMorris " the Irishman, " Jamy " the Scotchman, and "Fluellen " the Welshman.

On reaching my studio one morning, while the streets were laid with ice and slightly concealed with snow, I said, " Mr. Ewing, you had a fall on your way," seeing that the snow still adhered to his overcoat, from his shoulder to his feet.

" Yes," he replied, " but no harm done, I hope."

Sure enough, and fortunately, too, no harm had befallen him, a man of almost gigantic proportions, for he was over six feet in height without his boots, weighed two hundred and sixty-four pounds, and was seventy years of age. Physically and mentally, for his years, he had not his peer in Ohio at that time. He was as straight as an arrow, and walked with a firm and decided step in coming to my room or while returning to his own residence.

While in Lancaster, many anecdotes were related to me of his physical prowess in his younger days.

The high leap was one of his best efforts in that line. Take two men, full six feet in height, and let them elevate a tape-line to the extreme height of their hands, and Mr. Ewing would clear it at a single bound.

I very rarely essayed to indulge in any freedom or passing compliment to Mr. Ewing. One day, however, I asked him his ethnological descent. He replied : " I believe I am of Norman-English origin." " I doubt it, Mr. Ewing." " How so ?" he enquired. " I believe you are of Etruscan descent. You doubtless remember,

Mr. Ewing, that the Etruscans were the first inventors of the dome; and as you have the finest dome I have ever modelled, you will, I hope, permit me to give you a place among the Etruscans."

There was one thing I loved about Mr. Ewing above all others: there seemed to be no malice or envy in his composition. He never expressed anything but appreciative kindness of all his professional brethren, East, West, North, or South. It is only your little minds that imagine the great are envious, and they are always looking out for the lion in the gate.

The society of Lancaster was very superior. There were no cliques or clans to disturb the harmony of the social circle. As there were no concert-halls or theatres at that time, except those in progress of erection, the citizens generally depended entirely upon their own accomplishments for their amusements.

When holidays came about, then each one vied with his or her neighbor in contributing to the entertainment and pleasure of all. Private theatricals, *tableaux-vivant*, music and dancing, the elephant and the dwarf orator, were sources at times of wild delight to the young masters and misses of the occasion.

In all of those innocent amusements no one participated more readily, with his presence and approbation, than Mr. Ewing. There are many of his accomplished friends and neighbors I would like to name in commemorating those happy socials.

Mr. Ewing himself was not thoroughly comprehended

or understood by the public. Like his own grand and lofty Mount Pleasant, with its bold and rugged front, which is inaccessible, with its wealth of sunshine and shadows; and yet there was, like that same beautiful mountain, an approachable side of his generous and noble nature that could be reached by the lowliest and humblest, the infant child, the loving maiden, and sterling manhood.

That the great State of Ohio is most fully represented on the "roll of honor" no one will dispute; and among those honored names, there is no one that stands out in bolder relief, in private and public estimation, for his many transcendent virtues, than the late Thomas Ewing.

T. D. J.

[Citizen and Gazette.]

SCHOOL-BOY DAYS OF THOMAS EWING.

BY ED. L. MORGAN.

The events of yesterday are not so fresh or legibly stamped upon my memory as the recollection of my first day at school; and I presume it was the first day for Tom Ewing and my elder brother, but Thomas had been previously taught to read in Dilworth's Spelling-book, his oldest sister being his instructor. It was a beautiful morning in the spring, I believe of 1799, my father as guide, in company with his charge, Thomas Ewing, my brother, John M. Morgan, and

myself, aged between five and six years, set out
for the new school-house which I have just described. The distance from home was about two
miles. Our path, for the most part, lay through
a thick wood, and we had to cross one fork of Short
Creek at about half-way. When we reached the creek,
my father took a great deal of pains to show and instruct us how and where to hide from the Indians,
if we should happen to see or hear them when on
our way to or from school.

On arriving at the school-house, we were duly introduced to the "master," whose name was John
Chambers, a Scotch Presbyterian, an old bachelor,
and a strict disciplinarian, both in school and in
church. Soon after our arrival, the master called
"books" with a loud, shrill voice, and the scholars,
who were mostly out at play, came pitching in, bare-
foot and bare-head, seated themselves on the rough
benches, and began reading in a loud voice; for that
was the fashion then, and he who could make the loud-
est noise, either in reading or spelling, was considered
the best fellow. Our school-book was Dilworth's
Spelling-book, and we all could read some in that
book, Thomas having been taught by his sister, and
my brother and I by our mother. At noon the
master read to us the rules of the school, and informed us of the different kinds and amount of punishment that would surely follow a wilful breach of
these rules. He also exhibited his instruments of tor-

ture, which consisted of a number of common whips, of different sizes, which had been cut from the branches of trees and thoroughly roasted in the hot ashes to make them tough. In one corner was the "dunce block," and over it, against the wall, hung the "dunce-cap" and the leather spectacles. A seat upon that block, with cap on head and spectacles on nose, was punishment for the lazy, inattentive sluggard who came late to school, and had no energy to learn when he got there. To one of the joists, immediately over the centre of the floor, was fastened a strong cord. This was used only in extreme cases.

Those who have used Dilworth's Spelling-book will remember that it contains many short quotations from Scripture. The following is one of them: "The wicked flee when no man pursueth, but the righteous are as bold as a lion." One evening, on our return from school, when we had got in sight of home, Thomas ran forward and called out, "Uncle! Uncle! I have turned over a new leaf." "Have you?" said my father. "Yes," said he, "I have turned over a leaf, and have got to the wicked *flea*." And he strutted round as proud as a peacock. It was one of the happiest days of his life, as I have heard him say forty years after.

One night that summer, there fell a heavy rain, and the next morning, my father, knowing the creek would be so high we could not cross it, directed us to ride an old gray horse which he had, and keep him at the school-house until evening, when we could ride home.

My brother, who was supposed to be the best rider took his position before; I, being the youngest, was placed in the middle, and Thomas behind, to hold me on. Thomas took the dinner-basket on his arm, and we started on our journey to school. (If I had a correct photograph of the old gray horse and his riders, it would cost something to buy it.) We had got across the creek, which was belly deep to the horse, when we discovered, as we supposed, that we had forgotten our dinner. We wheeled to the right-about, crossed the creek a second time, rode up to the door, called to mother, and told her we had forgotten our dinner; when, on coming out, she saw the basket of dinner hanging on Thomas's arm.

My father's library at this time consisted of but few books. The most prominent among them were the Bible and Testament, the *History of Greece*, Homer's *Iliad*, *Sandford and Merton*, *History of England*, *Æsop's Fables*, etc.

By the time the next winter had come, we had all made considerable progress in learning. Thomas and my brother had both got to be good readers, and one or the other always stood at the head of the "spelling class." They spent much less time at play than is common with boys, and were almost constantly engaged in reading or studying their lessons. When the long nights of winter came on, it was necessary to have artificial light, in order to continue our studies of evenings. For this purpose, on our return from school in the evening, we would each collect by the way and carry home an armful of bark, taken from the "shell-bark hickory," which, being put into the log fire of the cabin in small quantities, made an excellent light, by which all in the house could see, whether they were employed in reading, writing, spinning, or picking cotton. My two schoolmates always spent the Sabbath in reading the Scriptures; for my parents were very strict about the observance of that day, and would not allow us to read any other book on Sunday. On a certain Sabbath, Thomas and my brother, not wanting to be disturbed or interrupted by me while reading their Sunday lessons, enticed me to go out into a lot where stood the corn-crib, and, after opening the door, they showed me a large ear of red corn, and urged me to go in and bring it to them. As soon as I got fairly into the crib, they closed the door, and locked me in. I remained in prison for some time, and, after several fruitless attempts to make my escape, I called several times to my father before he heard; and when he came to my relief and heard my story, he got a good whip, and hurried to the house, determined to give the offending boys a flogging; but on his arrival, he found them reading, in a solemn manner, verse about in the Old Testament. This appeased his wrath in some measure, and they got off without bodily punishment.

About the year 1802 (I am not certain as to the pre-

cise time), Thomas Ewing went to live with his father's
family on Federal Creek, Athens County, Ohio, and
worked upon the farm for some time.   He afterwards
went to work at the Kanawha salt-works.   There, by
the light of the furnace fires at night, he pursued his
studies.   After his father's farm was paid for, and he
had laid by a few dollars, he entered the college at
Athens.   A short time before he went to college, he paid
a visit to my father's family on the Pan-Handle, and con-
sulted his uncle and aunt about the propriety of going
there.   They advised him to go if he thought he could
pay his way by his own labor, as his father, now in his
old age, could not assist him.   He had been but a short
time at Athens, when his funds gave out, and he again
went to work at boiling salt.   In this way he managed to
get through college, and was, I believe, the first graduate
of that institution.   Shortly after he finished his studies
at college, he commenced the study of law with Philemon Beecher, at Lancaster, Ohio, and that place was his
home ever after, until the time of his death, in October,
1871.

Soon after he had finished the study of law (which I
think was in 1816), he made a visit to my father's family, who then lived on King's Creek, a few miles north-
east of Urbana.   He was in search of a place to commence the practice of his profession, and had a consulta-
tion with my father about the propriety of locating in
Urbana; but, as we had lived but two years in the
vicinity of that place, my father was not sufficiently

acquainted with the country nor with its inhabitants to give a satisfactory opinion. My father being unwell, I accompanied Mr. Ewing to Urbana. I had but few acquaintances there at that time. We "put up" at the tavern of James Robison, stayed there and about town all day, and went home in the evening. The next day, Mr. Ewing concluded to go back to Lancaster, as he got no encouragement to locate at Urbana. When he set out on his return, I accompanied him to Urbana, and he stayed a couple of hours at the tavern, when he set out on his journey home. There were a goodly number of the citizens assembled at the tavern on the last day that he was there. Among the rest, I remember two who were practising lawyers and one law student. William Bridge, well known to all old settlers, was also present. After Tom had mounted his horse and rode off, the wise men of the company present began to criticise his character and appearance. Many were the sarcastic remarks about his personal appearance and his coarse, home-made apparel. It was agreed by nearly all present that he would never have talent enough to earn his living by the practice of the law, and that he would do better to return to the salt-works. The law student, who of course considered himself the wisest man in the company, said that any person of common sense could tell by the appearance of his head that he was, and always would be, nothing but a conceited "booby." At the close of the conversation, William Bridge, who had thus far been silent, made the following quotation from Burns:

" There's many a ragged colt been known
   To make a noble aiver;
   So he may some day fill a throne,
   For all your clish ma claver."

It is true he never filled a throne, but he occupied
stations of far more importance to the American
people. From this time forward his history is well
known.

I have in my possession a number of letters written
by Mr. Ewing, some to my father, and others to me.
I have now before me one directed to my father, and
dated Lancaster, August 4, 1818, from which I make
the following extract:

" I am still pleading law in Lancaster, and find it a
tolerably good business. My tutor, General Beecher,
who is our present member of Congress, is a candidate again at the ensuing election. Should he succeed, he will throw all his business into my hands,
which will establish me in a very lucrative practice.
You may conclude, therefore, that I am somewhat
anxious for his success. But aside from this, he is a
man of great talents and unimpeachable integrity, and
of political principles which you would not disapprove.
I hope you will give him your support. My love to
aunt, sister, and cousins; and believe me, with respect,
your nephew,   T. EWING."

It would be hard to make many of the citizens
of this county believe that at that time the counties

of Fairfield and Champaign, the towns, now cities, of
Lancaster and Urbana, were then included in the same
Congressional district; yet such is the truth. I will
now give a copy of another letter, dated thirty-eight
years later, and after he had retired from the arena
of politics:

"LANCASTER, Oct. 24, 1856.

"MY DEAR SIR: I have yours of the 20th, and,
like you, I am slow to learn the tricks of our new
political parties. I cannot vote for Buchanan nor
Fremont, for reasons which you will readily appreciate;
nor can I vote for Fillmore, for, although once a Whig,
he has abandoned the Whig party, and become a
Know-Nothing, of which I know nothing that is good,
and much that is evil. I will therefore give no vote
at the coming election.

"I am very truly yours,

"T. EWING."

The last time I met Mr. Ewing was on the cars
at Urbana. He was on his way home from Indian-
apolis, and it so happened that we both entered the
same car at the same time, but at different doors—
one at each end—and we eyed each other pretty
closely, each being doubtful of the identity of the
other. When we met near the middle of the car, I
ventured to hold out my hand, and say, "Tom Ewing,
I believe." He replied, "It is; and I believe this is
Ed. L. Morgan." He said our meeting reminded him

of a couple of Irishmen, who, soon after their arrival in America, happened to meet one day, and each supposed he knew the other; but they soon found they were mistaken, and had never seen each other before, when one of them said, "I thought it was you, and you thought it was me; but, by jabers, it is neither of us."

SALEM, November 20, 1871.

MISCELLANEOUS.

The following, from a Washington correspondent, is the only printed notice I have retained of the draping of the public buildings:

"THE LATE HON. THOMAS EWING.—As a mark of respect to the memory of this distinguished statesman, who died at his residence in Lancaster, Ohio, on Thursday afternoon last, in the eighty-first year of his age, the executive departments of the Government in this city were yesterday closed and appropriately draped in mourning."

The extract below, from the Cincinnati *Commercial*, I preserve, as it gives evidence that, in conformity with the Scriptural admonition, he avoided both poverty and riches; and, although commanding the means of wealth, he yet occupied his heart in the pursuit of higher aims and pleasures:

"The estate of the late Thomas Ewing amounts to about a hundred thousand dollars. A few years before his death, he distributed liberally among his children, the homestead falling to the share of his son, Thomas Ewing, Jr., who has since greatly improved it by remodelling the dwelling and beautifying the grounds. About one-half

of the estate was invested in stocks and bonds, and the
residue in real estate, chiefly in the coal and salt regions
of the Hocking Valley."

As a matter most interesting to us, their children,
and to our children and our children's children, I herewith give copies of the marriage record of father and
mother :

[Copy.]

Ewing   I do hereby certify that, on the 7th Jan'y,
to   1820, I solemnized the marriage of Thomas
Boyle.   Ewing and Maria W. Boyle.

EDWARD FENWICK, P. G.

—*Record of Marriages, Fairfield County, Ohio, No.* 1,
p. 179.

[Copy.]

"Thomas Ewing and Maria Boyle were married on
the 7th day of January, A.D. 1820."

The above is from the family Bible, in father's own
handwriting.—E. E. S.

The articles given below, from the *Catholic Telegraph,*
need no introduction from me :

DEATH OF THE HON. THOMAS EWING.—We learn with
heartfelt satisfaction from the newspapers, East and
West, the exalted esteem in which the life, virtues, and

services of the late Hon. Thomas Ewing, of Lancaster, were everywhere held, and the splendid tributes rendered to his memory by the most distinguished men and bodies of men in the nation. Equal in ability to his compeers in the Senate of the United States, it is no disparagement to them if we avow the truth of his having surpassed them in personal merit. Not one of them has left such an example to be admired and imitated by young men and old, by the private citizen and the public functionary; no one whose record is, in every respect, so bright.

Mr. Ewing, as his letters in our possession prove, always declared his conviction of the claims of the Catholic Church to be the one only true Church of Christ. In her communion, he beheld all the means of salvation instituted by the Saviour. To her he acknowledged our indebtedness for the only true civilization. In his admirable wife, he had daily before his eyes for forty-five years the type of every womanly Christian grace and excellence; and to her, unnamed in his eulogy, we believe he was greatly indebted for much of the success he achieved in his glorious career.

The book which Mr. Ewing read with most pleasure and profit, next to the New Testament, was the *Following of Christ*, by Thomas à Kempis, of which the Archbishop, years past, presented him a copy, and from this pure fountain of Catholic devotion he derived lessons of heavenly wisdom nowhere else better taught.

In his funeral oration, the Archbishop expressed the
34

wish that every young man would read and ponder on
the biography of Mr. Ewing, which, he said, deserved to
be written in letters of gold.　We repeat the wish, and
recommend the obituary contained in one of our city
papers, the day after his demise, to be inserted in our
school-books for the instruction of youth.

Hon. Thomas Ewing.—The last great act of this truly
great man was his profession of the Catholic faith and
reception of the Holy Sacraments.　It might seem to
some who knew him not as his children and his intimate
friends knew him, that this step, because so long deferred,
was at last hastily taken.　But this is not so.　It was
the subject of serious meditation, especially after his
marriage, fifty years past, with his late admirable Catholic wife.　During that long interval, he frequently declared his conviction of the truth of the Catholic
religion.　And yet, from an exalted, perhaps we may
say an exaggerated, sense of his responsibility to God
and man for his final determination, he still lingered on
the threshold of the temple—still anxiously disciplined
his mind and feelings before his solemn approach to the
altar.　Last December, when Archbishop Purcell went
to Mount Vernon, Ohio, for the marriage of his son,
General Charles Ewing, to an elegant and accomplished
young lady of that city, he addressed a letter to Mr.
Ewing, urging earnestly and respectfully his entrance
into the one fold of the one Heavenly Shepherd.　To
this letter, written by the Archbishop, as he stated in it,

after Mass, after placing his forehead in the dust, on his
knees on the vigil of the festival of the unbelieving and
believing St. Thomas, Apostle, he received the following
reply:

"MOUNT VERNON, Dec. 20, 1870.

"MOST REVEREND AND DEAR FRIEND:

"I regret that I cannot accept your suggestions, but I
have difficulties which you, educated in the faith from
childhood, can hardly appreciate.

"I am satisfied that the Christian religion is the
greatest boon, moral and social, that ever heaven bestowed on man. This is to me the highest evidence of
its truth, which would be lost if we repudiate the Catholic Church, by which it was originally taught and has
been transmitted through ages.

"Its doctrines and their proofs have been for some
years, and are still, my study; but my convictions are not
as unwavering as I could desire them, and I must be sincere before God and man and have full faith before I
make avowal.

"With sentiments of the highest respect and esteem,
I am,

"Your lifelong friend,

"T. EWING.

"Most Rev. Archbishop Purcell, present."

The second paragraph of this beautiful letter covers
the entire ground. The light so long sought and so fre-

quently implored was granted in his last hours, and he died a true believer.

COMMUNICATED.—"WESTERN CHRISTIAN ADVOCATE" OF 15TH NOVEMBER.—THE LATE SENATOR EWING.— The editors of the *Catholic Telegraph* charitably ignore, as a general thing, the scurrilities of the *Western Christian* (Methodist) *Advocate*. Here is a sample of one of these scurrilities not to be overlooked. Alluding to the High Mass by Rev. Mr. Young, and the sermon of Archbishop Purcell, at Mr. Ewing's funeral, the *Advocate* says:

" It may not be so generally known that the occasion was employed to eulogize the Romish Church, to the shameful neglect, if not positive insult, of the memory of the distinguished citizen, over whose senseless body mummeries were performed and statements made that in any rational hour of his former life he would have spurned with contempt."

" Nema," whose name is signed to the foregoing, forgets, if he ever knew, that Mr. Ewing, seven years past, " in a rational hour of his former life," invited Archbishop Purcell, not to perform what the *Advocate* impiously calls " mummeries," but to offer the adorable sacrifice of the New Law over the remains of his saintly wife, and to preach her funeral sermon, at both of which Mr. Ewing reverently assisted, far from spurning them with contempt. In using this vile language, the *Advocate* insults at once the virtuous living and the honored dead of Mr. Ewing's family. Will the *Advocate* atone by publishing Mr. Ewing's letter of the 20th December, 1870, to Archbishop Purcell?

Hon. John A. Bingham, of Ohio, has been kind enough to allow me to copy an interesting letter which my father addressed to him in 1870:

WASHINGTON, May 7, 1870.
MY DEAR SIR:

I thank you for the book you were kind enough to bring me. I am familiar with the works of John Stuart Mill, and think him one of our most profound thinkers and able logicians. In this Mr. Buckle has done him no more than justice.

The passage to which you specially called my attention —the proof of the immortality of the soul deduced from our love of family, associates, and friends while they live, and remaining after their death—has always had much weight with me, though it is an argument resting on feeling rather than reason, and is used by poets much more than by philosophers and theologians. Campbell embodies it in these brief lines:

> " If faith unite the faithful but to part,
> Why is their memory sacred to the heart ?"

Another argument deduced from our common nature,

and wholly independent of direct revelation, or creed, or forms of faith, is ,the universal feeling of immortality in all men, wheresoever found and in whatever age. Peoples and sects differ widely as to the state of the soul after death; but all agree as to its existence. The Buddhist and the Egyptian priest believed in its transmigration; the Gheber in its absorption into the divine essence; and the Arab, as represented by Job, that after death in our flesh we shall see God. But forms of· belief are unimportant to the argument; the *feeling* is and always has been universal, whether in hope or fear, and is wholly beyond the range of reason. It is in man as in the insect —a blind, unreasoning impulse, such as impels the worm to wrap itself in its cocoon preparatory to its resurrection as a butterfly. And surely in all that concerns us, in which our reason cannot guide to truth or lead to error; in all things which reason cannot grasp, we are in the hands of God as fully as the meanest things in creation, and are as sure to be truly informed by our feelings as they by their instincts. My individual feeling on that subject is too strong to leave a doubt. I can no more conceive a possibility of my *future* than of my *present* non-existence; and I do not fear disappointment, for as to the. general fact of a future state, it is certain I can never know myself to have been mistaken.

If we analyze the feelings of men who profess to be unbelievers, we will find in their unpremeditated expressions enough to prove a feeling of their own immortality. Byron, suffering under his own wayward wildness, and "the stings and arrows of outrageous fortune," says, or makes his Giaour say for him,

> "I feel a wish within my breast
> For rest, but not to feel 'tis rest."

And elsewhere, in speaking of death, he calls it

> "That sleep the loveliest, for it dreams the least,"

but carrying with it always the feeling of an ever-existent Ego, to enjoy the rest and sleep the sleep. So the sceptic Mirabeau, after a strong and impassioned life, breathed out these words, the last that he uttered :

> "Now I sink to eternal sleep."

And the *I*, the *self* of which this eternal sleep is predicated, must be also eternal, or the expression were a paralogism, of which this master of language and logic was never guilty. All these seem to me to indicate, not an *opinion*, but a *feeling* of personal immortality.

Horace, one of the wisest and most genial of the Romans of the Augustan age—a gentleman with whom we would like to take a dinner and a social glass of wine—claims for himself immortality; he says :

> "Non omnis morior ; multa pars mei,
> Vitabit libertinam."

Though he grounds his claim to immortality on thoughts

which he had already uttered, it is *he*, Horace, that is immortal.

And Mr. Buckle is right in saying that the burden of proof rests on those who deny the immortality of the soul. We know of its present existence by more immediate evidence than we know of the existence of the material world. We have our knowledge of the soul from self-consciousness, and of the material world through the cognition of the soul. We feel and know that the soul is living, and no man ever saw or knew it to die. The philosopher, therefore, who *affirms* must *prove* it to be mortal.

I sat down to write you a letter, and I have written almost a treatise. I send the book to the Library, and am,

Very truly yours,
[Signed]   T. Ewing.

Hon. John A. Bingham,
          House of Representatives.

The letter which follows was addressed to my brother after father had read, at his request, Mr. J. Huntington's admirable book, *Gropings after Truth:*

[Copy.]

Washington, May 3, 1870.

Dear Charles: The strongest evidence in my mind of the divine origin of Christianity is its effect on the civil-

ization of the countries in which it prevailed—its full
effect—the institution of families and the emancipation
of woman, and her elevation in the social scale. This
distinguishes Christian civilization from that of all
other peoples and religions, and it evidently had its
origin in the dogmas of the Catholic Church, the
Virgin Mother, and the Holy Family. These produced their full effect within the first fifteen hundred
years of our era, before Luther, or Calvin, or Henry
the Eighth lived, and was too well established for the
most potent of them to reform it. And this was not
due to the *degree* of civilization but to the institution
of Christianity. At the time of the Crusades, the
Mahometan populations of Asia were, as compared
with our rude ancestors, in a high state of civilization, and women were toys or slaves, and denied immortal souls. Indeed, under all other systems, the
advance of civilization failed to improve, and generally
made worse their condition. In the age of Homer,
they were more elevated and honored than in that of
Socrates and Plato; but from the earliest ages of the
Christian church down to the time of the Crusades,
their condition was elevated and honorable, and
during the ages of chivalry they were objects almost
of adoration.

"On Heaven and on your Lady call."

But the sober judgment of the church corrected
excesses and still held the family tie sacred and the

sex in due honor. We owe, therefore, to the Catholic Church the institution of families and the elevated social condition of woman. This is omitted as an argument in the little book you brought me.

Your loving father,

[Signed]   T. Ewing.

Gen. Charles Ewing.

Among the early missionary priests to whom my brother makes reference in the correspondence which follows, I well remember Fathers Martin, Miles, and Allemany, of the Dominican Order, the second of whom died Bishop of Nashville, and the latter is now Archbishop of San Francisco.

Dr. Munos, a Spanish priest, was a most interesting and learned man, whom my father entertained in early days, and often quoted in later ones, but whom I do not remember.

The memory of a Rev. Mr. Hill was also cherished in the family. He had been an officer in the British army, and, being converted to the faith, he abandoned all, and devoted his life to missionary labors.

In later years, Rev. Joshua M. Young, a native of Maine and a convert, and Rev. H. Lange won our love and reverence as devoted pastors, and enjoyed the high esteem and most affectionate regards of my father. They, too, have gone to their reward, the former having been appointed to the see of Erie some years before his death.

LANCASTER, O., March 5, 1872.

MOST REV. J. B. PURCELL, *Archbishop of Cincinnati:*

MY DEAR SIR: I have already told you that only a few days before his death, my honored father expressed to me his earnest desire to leave some token of his appreciation of the services of the early priests of the diocese of Cincinnati in assisting, by instruction and example, in forming the character of his children, and bringing them up in the way they should go.

This thought was much in his mind, and very often, in the last few years of his life, he gave expression to his sentiments of esteem and regard for this pious, self-sacrificing, and accomplished body of priests, with whom he had been brought in contact, and many of whom had often been his guests, and were endeared to him by the associations of the most intimate social intercourse.

It happened, as you know, in the good providence of Almighty God, that Father Dominic Young, almost the very last survivor (except your honored self) of this estimable band, came a welcome messenger to minister to him in what alone was needed to add to his lifelong exemplification of all the natural virtues, and prepare him for the supernatural life that was opening·before him.

He expressed some embarrassment in designating the specific object to which to direct the donation that he contemplated, but finally directed that it should be placed in your hands and left to your discretion.

I hope you will not deem it presumptuous in me to suggest that I think I but anticipate your own decision, and feel sure you will respect his views and wishes, if it is applied to the use of the Seminary for the education of priests to succeed the good fathers in grateful memory of whom it is bestowed.

Enclosed please find a draft for one thousand dollars, being the amount designated by my father; and I add in the name of the family a draft for one hundred dollars to cover the expenses of your visits to Lancaster on the occasions preceding his death, and for the funeral; which kind attentions are, I assure you, remembered with heartfelt gratitude.

With most affectionate and dutiful regard and esteem, I am, my dear Archbishop,

Your son,

P. B. EWING.

CINCINNATI, OHIO, March 7, 1872.

HONORED AND DEAR FRIEND:

Your much-prized letter, with its valuable contents, reached me on the 5th inst.

I have handed the thousand-dollar check to the President of the Seminary, with directions to have a solemn Mass of requiem offered at the Seminary for the repose of your honored father's soul, his name inscribed on the seminary tablet as a special benefactor, and his descendants gratefully commemorated in the holy sacrifice.

The one hundred dollars so generously destined for me, with your permission, I shall send to our venerated friend, Rev. Mr. Young, who was the happy chosen instrument, in the hand of God, to bring your lamented father into the church, on whose threshold he had lingered so long, and toward whose altar he had so long wistfully looked. This disposition of the one hundred dollars, I think, is most acceptable to your dear father and to all the family.

Profound respects to Mrs. Ewing, and blessings to the children. Kindest regards to all.

Yours, sincerely,
J. B. PURCELL,
Archbishop of Cincinnati.

The letters given below were written at a time when father was stricken suddenly ill in the Supreme Court-room at Washington, and thought to be beyond hope of recovery. As the perusal of them touched his tender heart, and warmed it toward the writers, I cannot refrain from giving them a place here:

LETTER FROM "OCCASIONAL."

(The following letter will appear in the Philadelphia *Press* to-day.)

WASHINGTON, October 22, 1869.

Thomas Ewing, one of the last of the old-school statesmen, has just been struck down in the Supreme Court

of the United States, and may not live over the night.
If he had chosen the place in which to close his honored
career, and the manner of his farewell, he would probably have selected the scene of so many of his noblest
triumphs. He was prostrated in the midst of an argument on an important land question. As I write, he lies
in one of the rooms adjoining the chamber of the Court
—that chamber to which, nearly forty years ago, he was
sent as a United States Senator by the Legislature of
Ohio, and in which for seven years he served as the
contemporary of Clay, Webster, Calhoun, Silas Wright,
Thomas H. Benton, W. C. Preston, George Poindexter,
John Forsyth, Martin Van Buren, James Buchanan, W.
R. King, Richard M. Johnson, James L. Southard, and
others, all of whom have gone before. He lived to a
greater age than any of these. Born on the 28th of
December, 1789, he is on the verge of eighty, having
lived longer than Clay, Webster, Calhoun, Wright, Benton, or Buchanan. He preserved his faculties to the last,
and the scene in the Court this afternoon, as described
by one of his eminent associates in the words which are
subjoined, must have been extremely impressive. He
has fallen literally in the harness. Time has dealt won-
derfully with him. Up to the last, he took a deep
interest in public affairs. The extraordinary vigor of his
mind is proved by the fact that he was contending in the
most trying of all theatres, with the ripest minds of his
profession. Within a recent period, he has contributed
to the newspapers on public questions. The kindest of

fathers, he was blessed in his children, four of whom came to his couch when he was carried from the Court. Few public men have lived so useful and so illustrious a career. He escaped the usual infirmities of old age. Good health, undimmed intellect, and a keen enjoyment of his great profession, he may be classed among the fortunate. If the story of his life is a grand lesson to his countrymen, the close of that life will add to the reverence with which his memory will be cherished.

Occasional.

Hon. Thomas Ewing, of Ohio, while arguing a case before the Supreme Court of the United States yesterday, fainted from nervous exhaustion, and, though partially recovering, is now lying in a dangerous condition at the Capitol.

Mr. Ewing was addressing the Court in the case of Tyler and Maguire—a writ of error to reverse the judgment of the Supreme Court of the State of Missouri, which came on by special assignment to be heard on a motion to refuse the mandate; Messrs. Curtis and Phillips for the motion, Messrs. Ewing and Carlisle *contra*. Mr. Ewing had taken part in the argument of the case in April last, which resulted in a judgment establishing the right of his clients, and the object of the motion was to modify that judgment. This involved a review of the case, in which Mr. Ewing felt great interest.

Yesterday, Mr. Phillips opened for the motion at 11 A.M., addressing the Court until 1 P.M., being followed by

Mr. Carlisle in opposition, who spoke until 2 P.M. Mr. Ewing then rose and spoke about fifteen minutes in a very clear and particularly animated manner. At the end of that time, he remarked to the Court that he did not feel so strong as he thought he would be when he commenced, and the Chief-Justice told him to continue his argument sitting. Mr. Carlisle placed a chair for him immediately facing the Chief-Justice, and Mr. Ewing walked around the counsel-table, and sat down. He had just begun to read from his brief, when, at the end of a sentence, he paused, and his head gently fell upon his shoulder. Mr. Carlisle at once saw that he had fainted, and rendered assistance, along with several of the judges on the bench, who came down for that purpose. Mr. Ewing recovered in a few moments, however, and told his colleagues to continue the argument. He himself, however, after a few minutes, rose to resume, but his lips refused utterance, his throat gave a nervous twitch, and he fell over. Medical aid was at once summoned—the 'Court adjourning—and Dr. C. M. Ford was the first to respond, Drs. Dove, Bliss, and Thomas Miller quickly following, rendering all aid in their power. Mr. Ewing's family was also sent for, he being removed in the meantime from the court-room to the private room of the judges. His two sons, General Thomas and Charles Ewing; his daughters, Mrs. General Sherman and Mrs. Steele; General Sherman, and Mrs. Admiral Dahlgren, soon arrived at the Capitol, and assisted as far as possible in alleviating his condition. Toward evening, he partially aroused from his lethargic state, and was conscious of the presence of those around him. It was deemed too dangerous by the physicians to remove him, and he remained at the Capitol all night. At 12 o'clock last night, his condition was much improved, and he had fallen into a sound sleep. His two sons, Thomas and Charles, Deputy Marshal of the Supreme Court Tisdale, and Dr. Miller were present with him. General Sherman left a few minutes before midnight. His friends hope he will be sufficiently recovered to permit of his removal to his residence this morning.

[Special Correspondence of the Cincinnati Gazette.]

HON. THOMAS EWING BEFORE THE SUPREME COURT—HIS SUDDEN SICKNESS, AND THE SUBSEQUENT SCENE.

WASHINGTON, October 23, 1869.

The scene in the Supreme Court-room yesterday, when Thomas Ewing lay before its bar, surrounded by the Court, his children, and many of his legal friends, all of whom believed him dying, was most solemn and impressive. It seemed as if the curtain which hides the past had been lifted, and events and persons long passed off the stage had returned. And when the first shock was over, there came to all who watched beside the unconscious old man thoughts of the days when, in the room where he lay, Webster, Calhoun, Benton, Clay, Buchanan,

Van Buren, Preston, Silas Wright, and King sat with him as senators nearly forty years ago. With power often, with brilliancy, with wit, with fluent and eloquent tongue, for many years he had played no common part among them; and now, on the very scene of their great efforts and renown, his death was calling back their times as no event has done since the war dug its great gulf between those days and these.

With the exception of the Chief-Justice and Justices Swayne and Miller, the Court, either in years or belief, belongs rather to the old times than the present. And Judge Curtis, who, in the case before the Court, was opposed to Mr. Ewing, was himself on that bench in the days of the Dred Scott decision. Mr. Ewing's associate, Mr. Carlisle, as Yerger's counsel, is pleading before the same tribunal for aid to roll back the new tides to which the wave gave motion. In the main, the scene was one of the past when Mr. Ewing rose to speak; for no one sits long at any time in the stillness of that court-room without having visions of the old senators. And except two or three lawyers of the new time, those around Mr. Ewing belonged to the old, and in their presence it was easier to recall those former days. The case was one which interested him deeply. He was acquainted with every element of it, as he had followed it as principal counsel for twenty-five years. Those who preceded him yesterday had occupied much time—much more than he had expected; and the old man, full of his subject, and hoping to end his case successfully after a quarter of a century of effort, rose at length, and, under his pent-up excitement, went on with a force and brilliancy that had caused those in attendance, who remembered his prime, to remark that his former strength in argument and his old eloquence had returned. The strength and elasticity of maturity seemed to return, and he held his command-ing figure for the moment as if in the enjoyment of full physical strength again. Thus he continued for near half an hour. It was while all eyes were on him that he sank exhausted. Old age settled over him again, as from his chair he continued his argument. And then a pause, and old age seemed to have yielded to death.

Hastily piling cushions in the area before the bar, they laid him down upon the theatre of so many years of labor. The Court adjourned and gathered around him, and for a time it was supposed that he was dead; and then for hours, although consciousness had returned, there seemed no hope of long sustaining life. Within an hour, quite an extended circle of family friends had arrived, to-gether with well-known surgeons and physicians of the District, and, with some of the most prominent members of the bar, all watched for several hours around the bed. The doors were closed, the room lighted, and there in the old Senate-chamber they waited for the old Senator to die.

Among those most affected was Gen. Sherman. In his person the present had its representative in that solemn scene; and while the past was for the hour so vividly recalled, he seemed the embodiment of that great army which had driven the chariots of war over it, and whose shoutings of victory had celebrated the birth of the new time.

For four hours there was no perceptible pulse-beat as this company watched, and in all that time only a few irregular flutterings of the heart, though consciousness came at times, when he could recognize his children and his associates.

In the evening, however, the rigorous measures used to restore brought him back from the very door of death, and at midnight he appeared almost out of danger again.

At midnight he was sleeping quietly, and most of those who had waited till they could feel assured that he would recover from the attack left the building. That midnight walk is one to be remembered by all who took it. The long, still corridors and the shadowy rooms ever brought back the Senate of half a century ago; and then the course of the sleeper as Secretary of the Treasury, as organizer of the Interior Department and its first Secretary, and then the long war, which settled so many of the questions which agitated the nation when the men of those days were in their prime, would crowd the mind. Coming out of the building, the long lines of white columns, still draped in mourning for Rawlins and for Pierce, looking still blacker in the moonlight, as if fresh shadows from the kingdom of death had fallen upon the drapery, and deepened the effect of the whole. Those who left felt, however much

they differed from him, that, if he were to die, it was
fitting he should be carried from the old Senate-chamber
to his tomb.

The many thousands of persons throughout our wide
republic who were grieved a few months ago on learning
that the venerable Mr. Thomas Ewing, ex-Senator and
ex-Secretary, had been suddenly stricken down by disease, never, as it was feared, to rise again, will be grati-
fied to learn that his stalwart form and noble and be-
nignant countenance are again familiar among us, and
that his clear mind and vast store of information and
gentle amenities are still the charm and delight of his
legions of friends.

Conclusion.

DEAREST and best, tenderest and truest of earthly fathers! thou friend of my mortal life, to whom my heart ever went forth in unselfish, absorbing devotion; whose love has cheered my every hour, and is with me still; smile now upon my accomplished task as thou wert wont to smile upon me here! No word or act of mine was ever deemed too weak for the kind, approving glance of thy sweet eye; no wilful, wayward expression e'er exhausted the fund of thy patient, loving forbearance. Engrossed by childhood's joys or pastimes, allured by youth's delusive pleasures, or weary with the cares of years, a child of thine found ever sympathy and comfort on thy dear bosom. Thy hand rested upon my head in benediction, or was held forth to guide and support.

Thou wilt not return to me, but I shall go to thee. Thy love greeted the dawn of my existence, and my soul will meet thee as it goes hence to its Creator; and there, in the day of resurrection, I shall again behold thy face, whose glorified beauty cannot express more than has ever been for thee the desire of the heart of thy child.

www.ingramcontent.com/pod-product-compliance
Lightning Source LLC
Chambersburg PA
CBHW031410270326
41929CB00010BA/1405